Recommendations

"Winfield Bevins' book on the life and ministry of John Wesley is a must-read for those who trace their roots to the Wesleyan-Pentecostal tradition. Understanding the man and his calling will foster a greater appreciation for our rich heritage as well as enhance our vision for the church of the future."

G. Dennis McGuire, General Overseer
Church of God, Cleveland, TN

"Everything old is new again! Reverend Winfield Bevins provides a fresh, accessible introduction to John Wesley, which can be used to mentor and coach a whole new generation of clergy and laity who are concerned about discipleship and church renewal, without sacrificing theological integrity."

Steven J. Land, President
Church of God Theological Seminary

"We are much indebted to Winfield Bevins for this inspiring book on the legacy and relevance of John Wesley. One of the main contributions of this book is that the connection between Methodism and Pentecostalism is clarified. Winfield is to be commended for making that link so clear and reminding us of our heritage.

Laurence W. Wood
Asbury Theological Seminary

To Brenda + Russell,

With Love,

[signature]

REDISCOVERING
JOHN WESLEY

REDISCOVERING
JOHN WESLEY

WINFIELD H. BEVINS

Unless otherwise indicated, Scripture quotations are taken from the *New King James Version*. Copyright 1979, 1980, 1982, 1990, 1995, Thomas Nelson Inc., Publishers.

Scripture quotations marked KJV are from the King James Version of the Bible.

Book Editor: Wanda Griffith
Editorial Assistant: Tammy Hatfield
Copy Editors: Esther Metaxas
Aimee Norton

Library of Congress Catalog Card Number: 2004116650
ISBN:1-59684-024-2
Copyright © 2004 by Pathway Press
Cleveland, Tennessee 37311
Printed in the United States of America

Table of Contents

Dedication

I dedicate this book to the
three women in my life:

My wife,

Kay,

our daughter,

Elizabeth Susanna,

and my mother,

Jane Lewis.

Without their love and support
I would not be where I am today.

Acknowledgments

Books are never written by authors alone but are often the result of other people who have influenced the author's life. I would like to thank the following people for helping me in the writing of this book: Dr. Steven J. Land, president of the Church of God Theological Seminary, for his wisdom and counsel; Dr. Larry Wood, for his time and consideration; Drew Landrus and Tony Ritchie, for reading the manuscript in its earliest form and suggesting that I submit it for publication; and to Rev. Corky and Dr. Kimberly Alexander, for their friendship and support.

I am also deeply grateful to the staff of Pathway Press, especially Bill George, editor in chief, for giving me the opportunity to share John Wesley with the Evangelical and Pentecostal family. I would also like to give special thanks to the men and women of the Crab Orchard Church of God for sharing their lives with me and allowing me to be their pastor. Last, but certainly not least, I would like to thank my wife, Kay, for her love and support during this endeavor.

Foreword

We are indebted to Winfield Bevins for this inspiring book on the legacy and relevance of John Wesley. One of Wesley's fundamental principles was to preach and write with simplicity and clarity so that all could hear and understand the gospel. Winfield Bevins is this kind of teacher and preacher. This is a forthright and reliable interpretation of the life and thoughts of Wesley in plain terms.

Some biographers of Wesley tend to romanticize him in a way that makes him to be more than truly human. While showing high respect for a man who was so singly devoted to the work of God, Winfield gives us a clear and balanced view of Wesley, the man and his message.

One of the truly remarkable things is that God uses "earthen vessels" as means of divine grace. Wesley was certainly such an earthen vessel who deserves the attention given to him in this book. More significantly, we need to learn about the great saints of the past as role models for us today. This is especially true of Wesley because he is our "father in God," a phrase he once used in conversation with the American Methodists.

An enduring feature of this book is that it summarizes, in brief scope, the essentials of Christian living and belief. Some of these themes, such as the new birth, entire sanctification and the Spirit-filled life, may seem commonplace to us today . . . perhaps too commonplace. Many people are not aware of how rare a proper understanding of these evangelical themes was in Wesley's day. Winfield rightly calls attention to these basic convictions and the need to be reminded of their significance for us today.

This is urgent for us today, because too many believers across all denominations are enjoying the good feelings that go along with the Christian life without giving adequate attention to the disciplined life of holiness. The book rightly calls us back to the basic meaning of Christian experience loving God with all our heart, mind and soul, and our neighbors as ourselves. This was the central theme of Wesley, and this is why he said that spreading "Scriptural holiness across these lands" is why God raised up the people called Methodists.

One of the main contributions of this book is that the connection between Methodism and Pentecostalism is clarified. Pentecostalism is as much a Methodist Movement as any denominational group in America. As Winfield shows, Wesley defined a Methodist as one who feels the special responsibility of being a witness to holiness of heart and life. Besides the fact that the Methodist Movement gave birth to the Pentecostal tradition in the early 1900s, Pentecostalism is known as a Holiness Movement primarily because of its Methodist message.

The word *Methodist* was first used derogatively to describe Wesley during his student days at Oxford University because of his unusual methods of promoting a disciplined life of holiness. When they have been true to their heritage, Methodists have always stood out as different from the world because of their method of exhibiting personal and social holiness through Bible study, fasting and ministering to the poor.

The problem is that today too many are Methodists in name only. Wesley said he never feared the day when Methodists would cease to exist, but he worried that one day Methodists would only have a form of godliness, while denying the power of God in their lives. The Pentecostal revival arose in large part to keep the spirit of original Methodism alive in the world, and it continues today as the fastest-growing Christian movement in the world. Wesley would surely consider himself to be the "father in God" of Pentecostals as he was to the early American Methodists.

Showing the connection between Pentecostalism and Methodism is an important step toward helping both Pentecostals and Methodists in general to understand their common roots. Winfield is to be commended for making that link so clear and reminding us of our heritage.

Laurence W. Wood
Professor of Systematic Theology
Asbury Theological Seminary
Wilmore, Kentucky

Introduction

There are millions of men and women who are spiritual descendants of John Wesley, but many of them know very little about him. The purpose of this book, then, is to introduce contemporary Christians to John Wesley to speak across the generations to Christians of all denominational backgrounds so that they may discover the vital contributions Wesley made, and continues to make, to the church today.

Steve Harper said: "Meeting John Wesley is like exploring an ocean; there are many ways to do it. You can wade in the shallows or dive into the depths. Either way there is enjoyment." You are invited on a journey to rediscover John Wesley. Perhaps you are learning about him for the first time, or you simply want to learn more about him. Either way, I am confident that you will find this study of John Wesley both encouraging and refreshing.

There are many books and articles that have been written about John Wesley, but few people really know the man and his impact on the church. Most of the writing concerning Wesley is too academic in nature and is not readily available to laypeople, especially those outside the Methodist tradition.

I do not believe that this is consistent with the way Wesley did theology. He desired "plain truth for plain people." Therefore, it is my intention to offer an introduction to the life, ministry and theology of John Wesley that is understandable, readable, applicable and practical.

This book is divided into four sections. The first section is foundational, discussing Wesley's life and ministry. Special attention is given to the relevance of the events and people that affected his life.

Section two addresses the main doctrinal themes of his message, with emphasis on his doctrine, theological method and concept of holiness.

The third section of the book considers Wesley's legacy and discusses the various Wesley offshoots—including the often-overlooked connection to the modern Pentecostal/Charismatic Movement.

Lastly, study aids are provided to help readers better familiarize themselves with Wesley's life and ministry.

Now let's meet John Wesley.

part one

John Wesley's
Life and Ministry

* * * * * * *

A CHARGE to Keep I Have

A CHARGE to keep I have,
A God to glorify;
A never-dying soul to save,
And fit it for the sky.

To serve the present age,
My calling to fulfil:
O may it all my powers engage
To do my Master's will!

Arm me with jealous care,
As in Thy sight to live;
And O Thy servant, Lord, prepare
A strict account to give!

Help me to watch and pray,
And on Thyself rely,
Assured, if I my trust betray,
I shall for ever die.

—Charles Wesley

chapter one

Wesley's Early Life

John Benjamin Wesley was born June 28, 1703, in the small town of Epworth in northern England. He was one of 19 children born to Samuel Wesley and Susanna Annesley. He was born into a family that had a wonderful heritage of ministry; his father, Samuel, was a parish priest and both of John's parents were the children of clergy. Samuel was the son and grandson of clergy and Susanna was the daughter of a clergyman. It seemed natural that John would follow in the footsteps of his father, grandfather and great-grandfather in the service of the Lord.

Early Life at Epworth

John's life at Epworth left a lifelong impression on him. Under the influence of his parents, he developed a love for the Church of England, education and devotion to God. Many people think Susanna had an even stronger influence on John than his father. She was well read—especially in religious literature. She kept up the household, taught and disciplined the children, and even held prayer meetings in the rectory when Samuel was away. Upon his mother's death in 1742, John recollected, "I cannot but further observe, that even she (as well as her father, and grandfather, her husband, and her three sons) had been, in her measure and degree, a preacher of righteousness."

On February 9, 1709, a fire began at the rectory just before midnight. Without a moment to lose, most of the family escaped down the staircase and out the window. To his dismay, Samuel discovered that John Wesley was still asleep. Samuel tried to get back into the house, but the fire was too violent. At the last minute, a man was set on another's shoulders to rescue John from the fire. Within only a few minutes from the time the fire started, the whole house burned to the ground. John would never forget the providence of God that saved him from the burning fire. His mother called him a "brand plucked out of the burning."

Wesley's Training

Wesley's formal education began in 1714, when he was sent to Charterhouse—a school that prepared him to enter Oxford University. He matriculated into Christ Church College, Oxford, in 1720. By the time of his graduation in 1724, he had become well read in theology, science, history and classical literature.

While at Oxford, John had only a seminal interest in religious matters, and he had no interest in inward religion. This began to change in 1725, which marked the beginning of John Wesley's religious awakening and the first of three phases in his theological development. When he considered entering the Church, his parents enthusiastically encouraged him.

During this time, several major things helped shape Wesley's religious thought. Wesley came into contact with Bishop Jeremy Taylor's *Rules and Exercises of Holy Living and Dying*, Thomas à Kempis's *Christian's Pattern*, and William Law's *Christian Perfection and Serious Call*. These writings made a profound impact on Wesley's spirituality, directing him to the path of holiness. Along with these selected readings, he took Communion every week, attended prayers, avoided outward sins and sought to live a holy life before God. On September 25, 1725, he was ordained a deacon in Christ Church Cathedral by Dr. Potter, bishop of Oxford.

The following year (March 17, 1726), Wesley was elected a Fellow of Lincoln College. Around the same time, his younger brother, Charles, had enrolled as a student at Christ Church. They joined a small group of Oxford students that met regularly for the purpose of spiritual formation. It was not long until John became the unofficial leader of the group.

Along with their academic pursuits, the group engaged in prayer, Bible study, fasting, Communion, and social work that included prison visitation and caring for the sick. It was these practices that earned them nicknames such as "Enthusiasts," "Bible Moths," "Sacramentalists," "Holy Club," and "Methodists," which in time became the title of the Wesleyan Movement.

Around this same time, an important alliance was formed between the Wesleys and George Whitefield, who would later become a leader in the Evangelical revival. Whitefield was a fellow student and member of the Holy Club. Wesley was impressed with his wit and piety. During this time, Wesley became acquainted also with ancient Christian literature. His love for the Eastern Fathers is seen throughout his *Works*. He became convinced that their pattern of holy living was true and authentic Christianity.

These influences marked Wesley's time at Oxford as an important season of religious development. A combination of selected readings, academic training and certain influential persons influenced Wesley the most during his Oxford years.

Trials in Georgia

In 1735, only eight weeks after their father's death, John and Charles Wesley set sail for Savanna, Georgia. They had been commissioned by the Society for the Propagation of the Gospel, the missionary wing of the Church of England. After a two-month trip by sea, the Wesleys landed on February 6, 1736.

John's purpose for traveling to America was to minister to the Indians, but he served as parish minister to the colonists in Savannah. Charles became the personal secretary to the colony's governor, James Oglethorpe. General Oglethorpe had been a friend of Samuel Wesley and was anxious to have the two sons in Georgia.

The mission in Savanna lasted less than two years. Their ambitions for coming to America were never fully realized. Charles' relationship with Oglethorpe was estranged from the very beginning. John's dreams of evangelizing the Indians were never fulfilled. He labored tirelessly among the colonials.

While there, he fell in love with one of the parishioners, Sophy Hopkey. A brief relationship followed, but John was not able to propose. Sophy became engaged to a Mr. Williamson. Five months after their marriage John refused to serve Communion to the new Mrs. Williamson. The Williamsons sued John for defamation of character. Finally, after several months, John wrote in his journal, "I saw clearly the hour was come for leaving this place."

On his way to Georgia, Wesley became acquainted with a group called the Moravians, German pietists who were associated with teachings of Count Nicholas Ludwig von Zinzendorf. The Moravians taught a simple faith and assurance of salvation through the inner witness of the Spirit. Wesley was impressed with the Moravians' confidence, piety and assurance of faith. On February 7, 1736, while in Georgia, a Moravian leader by the name of August Gottlieb Spangenburg began to question Wesley's faith. Wesley recounts the dialogue:

> "My brother, I must first ask you one or two questions. Have you the witness within yourself? Does the Spirit of God bear witness with your spirit, that you are a child of God?" I was surprised, and knew not what to answer. He observed it and asked, "Do you know Jesus Christ?" I paused, and said, "I know he is Savior of the world." "True," replied he; "but do you know he has saved you?" I answered, "I hope he has died to save me." He only added, "Do you know yourself?" I said, "I do." But I fear they were vain words.[1]

This was instrumental in leading Wesley to search for an inward Christianity of the heart. On the way back to England, he wrote, "I went to America to convert the Indians; but oh, who shall convert me? Who is he that

will deliver me from this evil heart of unbelief?" No
doubt this was written in comparison with the assurance that Wesley witnessed among the Moravians.

When Wesley returned to England, he spent several
months in spiritual distress and deep introspection.
He was challenged by the example of simple faith in
Christ the Moravians had demonstrated before him.
In England, John and Charles met Peter Böhler,
another Moravian, who convinced John further that
conversion happened in an instant and that a real
Christian would have an assurance of salvation. He
testified to this experience and brought Wesley several
other witnesses who testified to the same experience.
While Böhler shared about the mercies of God, Wesley
began to weep—determined he would seek full assurance of salvation.

> I was now thoroughly convinced and, by the
> grace of God, I resolved to seek it unto the end,
> first, by absolutely renouncing all dependence,
> in whole or in part, upon my own works of
> righteousness—on which I had really grounded
> my hope of salvation, though I knew it not, from
> my youth up.[2]

The Moravians' impact on Wesley cannot be over-
estimated. Herbert McGonigle stated, "No group of
Christians had helped John Wesley more sincerely or
more profoundly than the Moravians."[3] In his journal
entries from April 2 to May 24, 1738, we can see how
the Moravians were instrumental in leading him to
search for an inward Christianity of the heart that was
accompanied by the inner witness of the Spirit.

From the Moravians he learned faith, assurance and Christian experience that are rooted in the experiential work of the Holy Spirit. Their lasting influence can be seen in Wesley's concept of the "witness of the Spirit" found throughout his writings, especially in his sermons.

Heart Strangely Warmed

On May 24, 1738, while attending a prayer meeting at Aldersgate Street in London, John Wesley had an experience that forever changed his life.

> In the evening, I went very unwillingly to a society in Aldersgate Street, where one was reading Luther's Preface to the Epistle to the Romans. About a quarter before nine, while he was describing the change which God works in the heart through faith in Christ, I felt my heart strangely warmed. I felt I did trust in Christ, Christ alone for salvation; and an assurance was given me that he had taken away my sins, even mine, and saved me from the law of sin and death.[4]

This experience was called by some people as Wesley's evangelical conversion. Albert Outler said, "It is as if Wesley came to realize that Aldersgate had been one in a series of the 'turning points' in his passage from don to missionary to evangelist."[5] Charles had a similar experience only three days before. Aldersgate was an important event in John's religious life that changed the course of his ministry.

To follow up on this unique religious experience, John traveled to Herrnhut, Germany, to visit the homeland of the Moravians. He hoped to solidify the work God had wrought in his heart. He conversed with their leader, Count Zinzendorf, and observed the lifestyle and religious practices of their community. At the time he seemed to be impressed with their unity and piety. However, only a few months after he returned to England, Wesley complained that they were too passive and did not exercise enough care in practicing the means of grace, such as prayer, fasting, Communion and Bible study. They overemphasized the internal witness of the Spirit and made assurance a requirement for salvation. This was the beginning of Wesley's rift with the Moravians.

Lessons for Today

The early life of John Wesley was marked by discipline, dedication and hard work. Many biographers attribute Wesley's disciplined lifestyle to his parents, Samuel and Susanna. Susanna in particular, made a tremendous impact on John's life. We cannot underestimate the influence parents have on the development of their children.

One of the lessons we can learn from Wesley's early years is that hard work and dedication certainly pay off in the long run. As a youth, he was dedicated and disciplined in every area of his life. Whether it was school, visiting the sick or teaching others, he was totally dedicated to the task at hand. The young Wesley stands out as a brilliant example of how one young person can make a difference in the world. There is truth in saying that "children are our future."

REFLECTION QUESTIONS

1. What is the most interesting thing you learned about Wesley's early life?

2. What seem to be the most influential events that happened to Wesley in this early stage of his life?

3. Who were the most significant people in Wesley's life, and why do you think they made such an impact?

4. Can you see any similarities with John Wesley's early life and other Christian leaders?

Endnotes

[1] Thomas Jackson, *The Works of John Wesley* (Grand Rapids: Baker, 1979) 1:23.

[2] Works, 1:102.

[3] Herbert McGonigle, *John Wesley and the Moravians* (England: The Wesley Fellowship, 1993) 24.

[4] Works, 1:103.

[5] Albert Outler, *John Wesley* (New York: Oxford, 1964) 52.

chapter two

The Rise of the Wesleyan Revival

George Whitefield experienced wonderful success in ministry with field preaching in the United States and England, but Wesley's new message of inward religion was not received well by the established Church of England.

In April 1739, George Whitefield convinced Wesley to preach in the open air in Bristol. John reflected in his journal, "I submitted to be more vile and proclaimed in the highways the glad tidings of salvation, speaking from a little eminence in a ground adjourning to the city about three thousand people."

This event marked the beginning of John Wesley's evangelistic ministry. From this time forward and with a new evangelistic zeal, Wesley took the message of Christ to everyone he met.

Societies

Although George Whitefield was a masterful preacher who led thousands to repentance and faith in Christ, he did not have the insight or leadership genius to place the new converts into a structured society for nurture and development. Wesley, on the other hand, saw the need to create a society for follow-up, fellowship and accountability. He learned the need to be in a discipleship group during his Oxford days with the Holy Club. All who desired to "flee from the wrath to come, and to be saved from their sins," were invited to join a society. Wesley believed that it was important for Christians to stay together. The Christian faith was a social religion. To turn it into a solitary one would destroy it.

Today, as a result of his message of social Christianity, Wesley left an enduring legacy for his spiritual descendants through the societies in every part of the world, while George Whitefield's name is hardly known. We cannot overlook the importance of discipleship and fellowship in Wesley's life.

The Methodist Movement began to spread through the British Isles. Wesley would appoint a lay leader to oversee the work in a society where believers had been gathered together. Wesley carefully chose and handpicked these lay leaders. They were men and women of piety and experience. This solidified the growth of the Movement. As a result, these societies began to multiply and continued to grow rapidly throughout England. Everywhere they went, societies were created to nurture new converts. The numbers of Methodists grew literally from a handful to thousands of followers at an amazing rate.

Because of the need for a location to accommodate the growing numbers of Methodist societies, Wesley felt the need to build Methodist chapels. The first one was called the New Room, in Bristol. This chapel served as a place of worship and also contained a living area for Wesley when he was visiting in Bristol.

In 1739, Wesley also purchased and remodeled an old factory in London called the Foundery, an important location for early Methodism. Along with having a residence for Wesley, it had a chapel for worship and an area for publishing Methodist literature. It served also as a location for various social ministries. Several other chapels were built for Methodist societies in various parts of England during this time.

Lay Preachers

As Methodism grew, Wesley saw the need to appoint lay preachers to assist him in preaching the gospel to the masses. This was a bold decision because it meant breaking from the traditional view that only the ordained clergy could preach the gospel. Some of these lay preachers were full-time ministers, while others ministered in their spare time. As the number of Methodist lay preachers grew throughout England, Wesley saw the need to organize the lay preachers.

In 1744, Wesley began annual meetings with his preachers to discuss the doctrine and discipline of Methodism and appoint preachers to their locations for the following year. This was the origins of the Methodist Conference. Here the preachers played an important role in the development of Methodism. This conference not only gave them a voice, but it also strengthened their support for Wesley's leadership, uniting them and giving them a sense of ownership for their ministry. Although the first conference only had a few in attendance, by the time of Wesley's death, there were hundreds of lay preachers.

It was never Wesley's intention to separate from the Church of England; rather, he believed that Methodism was a renewal movement within the Church. However,

the organization of the general conference of the preachers would ultimately result in the separation between
the Methodist and the Anglican Church. As time went
on, the Methodists became increasingly alienated from
the Church of England. By the time of Wesley's death in
1791, virtually all ties were broken between the
Methodists and the Anglican Church.

Methodism Comes to America

Despite opposition, Methodism continued to grow
and flourish within the British Isles. Methodism was
destined to spread like wildfire beyond the borders of
England. In 1760, Robert Strawbridge and his wife,
Elizabeth, moved from Ireland to America and became
the first Methodist pioneers in the New World.
Strawbridge established the first organized Methodist
society and meetinghouse in Maryland near Baltimore.

John Evans is thought to be the first Methodist convert in America under Strawbridge's ministry.
Strawbridge is also known for his controversial decision to administer the sacraments as a lay minister.
His pulpit in Baltimore, Maryland, is the oldest exist-
ing Methodist pulpit in America.

In 1766, Philip Embury and Barbara Heck, two
cousins who were Irish Methodist, formed a
Methodist class in New York City. Embury, converted
under Wesley's ministry, had been a lay preacher in
Ireland. Seeing the need for a society in New York,
Heck convinced Philip to begin preaching again. Only
six attended the first meeting, but it soon grew into a
large meetinghouse called the Upper Room.

Embury organized two more classes, which were
racially mixed, but sat separately. A British army offi-
cer, Thomas Webb, came to America to assist the work

in New York. He helped to raise finances for the church. Webb was also committed to spreading the gospel in other areas, and in 1767 he organized the first Methodist group in Philadelphia. In 1769, in response to a letter from Thomas Taylor asking to send "an able, experienced preacher," John Wesley sent Richard Boardman and Joseph Pilmore to serve as his assistants in America. Two years later, Wesley sent two more preachers, Richard Wright and Francis Asbury to assist the work. In 1773, two more preachers, Thomas Rankin and George Shadford were also sent.

These early Methodist lay preachers were men of deep Christian devotion and holy living. They were committed to spreading the Methodist message of God's love and holiness throughout the Colonies. Under their leadership, Methodism continued to grow steadily.

Division and Difficulty

The following years were full of both trials and great triumphs. Methodism made great strides toward reviving authentic Christianity. However, as Wesley's movement began to grow, so did persecution. In many cities he and his preachers were met with great opposition. Mobs tried vigorously to stop the Methodists from spreading the message of Scriptural holiness throughout the British Isles. Time after time, Wesley's life seemed to be spared by some type of divine intervention. Stories abound where it seemed the crowds might take John's life, but he would be spared from harm by some odd occurrence.

Although Methodism encountered a great deal of physical confrontation, perhaps the most vehement opposition came in the form of the theological controversies that arose from Wesley's gospel of free grace.

Nowhere was this felt more strongly than within Methodism itself.

There were two camps within Methodism—the Calvinists and Arminians. George Whitefield was the leader of the Calvinists. *Calvinism*, developed by reformer John Calvin, teaches . . .

- All humanity is depraved.
- There is unconditional election for the saved.
- The Atonement was limited to the chosen.
- God's grace is irresistible.
- The saints will persevere to the end.

This was in conflict with Wesley's doctrine of free grace (Arminianism), which believed that salvation was available to all men and women—not just the elect. "Whosoever shall call on the name of the Lord shall be saved" (Acts 2:21). This was not to say that humanity is good in any way, but that God's prevenient grace is extended to everyone who chooses or refuses to believe the gospel.

Another point of contention was with the controversy that came from enthusiasts who emphasized religious feelings and emotionalism. Wesley had to defend his movement from critics who accused them of being enthusiasts—emphasizing the emotional nature of Christianity. Wesley wrote several letters and sermons to defend Methodism from these charges. He felt that these accusations were unfair to the overall nature of Methodism and spent a considerable amount of time and energy defending the Movement.

A sect of enthusiasts actually broke off from Wesley's Methodists. One of their leaders was Thomas Maxfield, one of Wesley's lay preachers. A deep rift was driven between Wesley and Maxfield over the enthusiast controversy. Part of the problem was because enthusiasts claimed to have the inner work of the Spirit without bearing the outward fruit of the Spirit. Therefore, Wesley instructed his followers not to fall into enthusiasm. He addressed these issues in his *Plain Account of Christian Perfection* and sermons on the *Witness of the Spirit I & II*.

John Wesley's days of courtship did not end with Sophy Hopkey in Georgia. In fact, his problems with women were only getting started. In 1748, John intended to marry Grace Murray, a Methodist widow who had previously been a housekeeper and was considerably younger. Charles Wesley did not approve of the relationship because he didn't believe she was the right woman for John, so he convinced her to marry another Methodist preacher by the name of John Bennet. Needless to say, John Wesley was very upset over the matter. The event was a big scandal and almost caused a lifelong division between the two brothers.

In February 1751, John hastily married Mary Vazeille, a wealthy widow. After several years of marriage they began to have serious problems. Wesley spent most of his time and attention working to promote the spread of Methodism. Mary became jealous of his tireless work and his close friendship with certain Methodist women. Her jealousy may not have been altogether unjustified. Wesley worked day and night and had little time for a stay-at-home wife.

John and Mary separated on several occasions. When she died, he was out of town and did not attend her funeral. This is perhaps one of only a few areas of Wesley's life that can be criticized. He was a faithful husband, but the sheer demand of the apostolic work he undertook would have put a strain on any marriage.

Lessons for Today

The Wesleyan revival gave many contributions to the church. His society structure can be found in many of our contemporary denominations. A part of his genius was to put new converts into these societies in order that they receive care, accountability and fellowship. Some examples of this influence can be seen in cell groups, ministry and accountability groups, as well as the group structure of the G12 church growth movement.

Wesley also allowed lay preachers to minister the Word of God. This was nothing short of revolutionary in Wesley's day when only ordained clergy could preach the gospel. As a result, he opened the door for the modern lay leadership movement in the church today. God uses both men and women, ordained clergy and laypersons to accomplish His plans on earth. This means that everyone can do something for God.

REFLECTION QUESTIONS

1. What events helped spark the Wesleyan revival?
   Which one do you think was most significant?

2. What do think about Wesley's use of lay preachers? Was he justified in using them?

3. What do you think about the organization of the
   Methodist Movement? Could your denomination
   benefit from this type of structure?

4. Describe the main doctrinal division that split the
   Methodist Movement. Was it an issue of essentials or opinion?

5. What do you think about the persecution Wesley
   had to go through? Describe what you think your
   reactions would be if you had to defend your
   faith against angry mobs.

chapter three

Wesley's Ministry Contributions

The purpose of this chapter is to look at John Wesley's ministry distinctive. Two hundred years have passed, yet his life, message and ministry still speak to us today with the same power and relevance it did then. Few men have left such an impressible mark upon church history. John Wesley was an evangelist, theologian and minister. In his day Wesley used evangelism, discipleship, education and social witness to advance the kingdom of God. He raised a great army of ministers and missionaries whose numbers today range in the millions. Those of us who are in the Wesleyan tradition can and should draw from his life and ministry to receive guidance and direction for ministry in the 21st century. As we look at his influence on the church, we see several important elements that we will examine.

John Wesley was an ordained Anglican priest who came to America in 1735 as a missionary only to return to England less than two years later in total brokenness. He wrote in his journals, "I went to America to convert the Indians; but, oh, who shall convert me?" Once he returned to England, he had an experience that would change his life and the course of history forever. Upon hearing a reading from Luther's preface to the Epistle to the Romans, he felt his heart "strangely warmed." The power of this experience served as the catalyst that helped to ignite the fires of the Great Awakening of the 18th century.

The genuine experience of faith in Christ moved him with compassion to do all he could to share this experience with others. One of his most famous quotes was, "I look upon all the world as my parish." This was not an exaggerated remark. Wherever he went, he preached that everyone could have a relationship with Jesus Christ. This went against the grain of the nominal Christianity of Wesley's day. He was accused of being an enthusiast because he believed and taught that a person could have a life-changing experience with the Lord.

It is important to understand that for Wesley, salvation meant a genuine change in the life of the believer. He said that there is a real, as well as a relative, change that takes place at the time of the new birth. The faith he so desperately wanted to share was a faith of the heart that was born out of direct communion with God. Wesley said, "It is most true, that the root of religion lies in the heart, the inmost soul; that this is the union of the soul with God, the life of God in the soul of man."[1]

Field Preaching

John Wesley had a deep sense of compassion for the peril of sinful humanity. He undoubtedly believed in a literal hell. If there be no unquenchable fire, no everlasting burnings, there is no dependence on these writings wherein they are so expressly asserted, nor of the eternity of heaven, any more than of hell. So that if we give up the one, we must give up the other. No hell, no heaven, no revelation.[2]

Sin was at the root of the separation between God and humanity. Therefore, sin must be eradicated. He said, "We know no gospel without salvation from sin." His understanding of a lost humanity without God drove him to share the message of salvation.

John Wesley's burden for the salvation of others led him to move outside of the traditional religious methods of his day. When the pulpits began to close to Wesley because of his message, he unwillingly took to field preaching. Being persuaded by his friend and fellow revivalist, George Whitefield, he began to preach in the open air in Bristol. "At four in the afternoon I submitted to be more vile, and proclaimed in the highways the glad tidings of salvation, speaking from a little eminence in a ground adjourning to the city to about 3,000 people."[3]

This was to be the beginning of a life of outdoor preaching. After being barred from preaching at the church at Epworth, Wesley once preached a sermon from the top of his father's grave.

This was radically different than what had ever been done in the history of the Church of England. No one preached outside the walls of a church building. Rather than hindering his ministry, this bold new initiative allowed the message to be heard by the ordinary people who would not attend church. Wesley took the message of salvation to the highways and hedges, and the people responded by the thousands. It was this model of preaching he and his followers engaged in throughout the British Isles and North America. They saw great success in winning converts. Missionary zeal burned in their veins as they shared the gospel truth and obeyed the Master's call to "go . . . into all the world, and preach the gospel to every creature" (Mark 16:15).

Wesley left a missionary legacy in which an army of lay preachers accepted the call to evangelize the world. He challenged his preachers:

> It is not your business to preach so many times, and to take care of this or that society; but to save as many souls as you can; to bring as many sinners as you can to repentance, and with all your power to build them up in that holiness without which they cannot see the Lord.[4]

This call rang out among generations of Methodists giving them a sense of urgency to win the lost. These ministers saw themselves as a missionary church. One such man who heeded the call from Wesley was Francis Asbury, who became a bishop to the United States. He too affirmed this missionary charge by saying:

> The Methodist preachers, who had been sent by John Wesley to America, came as missionaries . . . and now behold the consequences of this mission. We have seven hundred traveling preachers, and three thousand local preachers, who cost us nothing. We will not give up the cause; we will not abandon the world to infidels.[5]

Class Meetings

The genius of Wesley was that he realized the importance of small-group ministry. He organized the people into class meetings to encourage and nurture believers in the faith. He knew that preaching was not enough to keep people in the faith. He wrote, "I determined, by the grace of God, not to strike one stroke in any place where I cannot follow the blow."[6] He followed the blow of salvation by putting people into these groups to make sure they kept growing in Christ.

Discipleship of new converts was important to John Wesley. He would have problems with our modern evangelistic crusades in which there is no follow-up or discipleship of the people who respond to the altar calls. Wesley warns, "Preaching like an apostle, without joining together those that are awakened, and training them up in the ways of God, is only begetting children for the murderer."[7] This was one of the major differences in the ministries of Wesley and Whitefield. At the close of his life, Whitefield lamented that he had not used the care of discipleship that Wesley had taken.

Wesley placed new converts into small groups that were designed to meet spiritual needs. They met weekly for prayer, instruction and mutual fellowship. Each group was about 12 in number, with one leader who was either a man or a woman. The leaders served their group with a kind of pastoral oversight. These groups met the various needs of the people who attended them.

He described these societies in the following way:

> Such a society is no other than a company of men having the form and seeking the power of godliness, united in order to pray together, to receive the word of exhortation, and to watch over one another in love, that they may help each other to work out their salvation.[8]

They were also admonished to do the following things:

1. Doing no harm and avoiding evil
2. Doing good of every possible sort
3. Attending upon all the ordinances of God, including prayer, sacraments, searching the Scriptures and fasting

Christians who were more spiritually mature became members of a band. The bands had fewer members and more rigorous requirements than the societies. The design was to provide a forum where each member of the group could confess his or her sins, encourage others, and pray for each other. The rules of the bands were as follows:

The design of our meeting is to obey that command of God, "Confess your faults one to another, and pray one for another, that ye may be healed" (James 5:16). To this end, we intend:

1. To meet once a week, at the least.
2. To come punctually at the hour appointed, without some extraordinary reason.
3. To begin (those who are present) exactly at the hour, with singing or prayer.
4. To speak each of us in order, freely and plainly, the true state of our souls, with the faults we have committed in thought, word, or deed, and the temptations we have felt since our last meeting.
5. To end every meeting with prayer suited to the state of each person present.
6. To desire some person among us to speak his own state first, and then to ask the rest, in order,

as many and as searching questions as may be, concerning their state, sins, and temptations.[9]

This account gives us a glimpse into what it was like to participate in one of these group meetings.

These groups were for the committed, although the general admission into these societies was to have a "desire to flee from the wrath to come, to be saved from their sins."[10] Wesley wanted the members to show constant progress in their walk with the Lord. There were guidelines by which the members were expected to adhere. Their spiritual progress was of the utmost importance. Meeting together regularly was a part of the process. Wesley exhorted them:

> Never omit meeting your Class or Band; never absent yourself from any public meeting. These are the very sinews of our Society; and whatever weakens or tends to weaken our regard for these, or our exactness in attending them, strikes at the very root of our community. As one saith, "That part of our economy, the private weekly meetings for prayer, examination, and particular exhortation, has been the greatest means of deepening and confirming every blessing that was received by the word preached, and of diffusing it to others, who could not attend the public ministry; where as, without this religious connection and intercourse, the most ardent attempts, by mere preaching, have proved of no lasting uses."[11]

Christians need discipleship that involves the whole body of Christ. There are no "lone rangers" in the kingdom of God. Wesley recognized the importance of

meeting together with other Christians to share experiences, holding one another accountable, and praying
for one another. The goal was for Christians to grow in
the faith and knowledge of the Lord Jesus Christ.
Spiritual progress was extremely important, which
involved interdependence with fellow believers.
Forming people into these groups was a successful
part of John Wesley's ministry contributions.

Education

Another unique contribution of John Wesley's
ministry was in the field of education. Personal piety
was not enough; he was committed to the process of
lifelong learning. The words of the hymn "Sanctified
Knowledge" by his brother Charles capture this integration of learning and piety:

> Unite the two so long disjoined,
> Knowledge and Vital Piety:
> Learning and holiness combined,
> And truth and love, let all men see
> In those whom up to Thee we give,
> Thine, wholly thine, to die and live.

Wesley promoted education to make his followers
more knowledgeable and his preachers more effective
in their ministry. He promoted the education of the
people called Methodists in the following ways:

1. *Wesley wanted to make Christian literature available to
every Methodist.* He did this by publishing hundreds of
books, pamphlets and other publications on a wide
range of topics that included poetry, history, grammar,
dictionaries and doctrine. He published his sermons,
letters, journals and his *Explanatory Notes Upon the New*

Testament. He also edited a 50-volume *Christian Library*, which included many Christian classics. The printed press was a means of spreading the gospel of Jesus Christ throughout the British Isles. He used the press to defend the doctrines of Methodism, to provide doctrinal guidance for his followers, and to address the various needs of the Movement.

2. *Wesley founded several schools in places where there was a strong Methodist presence.* He wanted to make education available to everyone. Wesley was particularly interested in the education of children. One of the most prominent schools was Kingswood School in Bristol, which opened in 1748. Students were required to maintain a rigorous schedule of study, which included philosophy, reading, writing, mathematics, science, music and theology. In addition they were expected to learn Latin, Greek, Hebrew and French.

3. *Wesley also supported the use of Sunday schools among Methodism.* A Methodist woman named Hannah Ball organized the first Methodist Sunday school in 1769. After Wesley's death, Methodists built numerous schools, universities, and seminaries around the world that remain in existence today.

Social Concern

John Wesley was concerned about the whole man. He sought to meet the needs of the individual, as well as to alleviate the evils of society. John and his brother, Charles, were moved by compassion for the lower class and disenfranchised people of society. They were not afraid to associate with others who stood for human rights. In a letter to William Willberforce, who fought against slavery in England, John Wesley wrote,

"O be not weary in well doing! Go on, in the name of the Lord God and in the power of his might, till even American slavery (the vilest that ever saw the sun) shall vanish away before it."[12]

John Wesley not only supported different social causes, but he was also actively involved in them. He used the societies as a means of "doing good" to others. Wesley urged his followers to actively participate in meeting the needs of those around them. He wrote:

> By doing good, by being in every kind merciful after their power; as they have opportunity, doing good of every possible sort, and as far as is possible, to all men: to their bodies, of the ability which God giveth, by giving food to the hungry, by clothing the naked, by visiting or helping them that are sick, or in prison; to their souls by instructing, reproving, or exhorting all they that have intercourse with.[13]

John Wesley was no hypocrite. He practiced what he preached. He often made 1,400 pounds a year from the sales of his books; however, he would only keep 30 pounds for himself. He gave his money to the poor and other worthwhile causes. He said, "If I leave behind me 10 pounds, you and all mankind bear witness against me that I lived and died a thief and a robber."[14] His denial of self and property for the sake of the less fortunate is very much like the early church, but is almost totally foreign in North America and Europe today.

Wesley believed the church should care for all of society especially those who could not take care of themselves. Believers have a social responsibility to the world. Wesley said: "Holy Solitaries" is a phrase no more consistent with the Gospel than holy adulterers. The Gospel of Christ knows of no religion, but social; no holiness, but social holiness. Faith working by love is the length and breadth and depth and height of Christian perfection.[15]

Lessons for Today

There is so much we can learn from the ministry of John Wesley. His ministry contributions can be applied to our present ministry situation whether it is in a local parish, a university or the mission field. His basic ministry strategy had to do with meeting the needs of the total person. Evangelism, or sharing the gospel, speaks to the human need of salvation from sin and death. It is a message of hope and healing. Genuine Christianity can be experienced by all who believe on the Lord Jesus Christ. This experience is open to all the people of the world regardless of their economic, racial, social or political background.

Discipleship and the gathering together of believers can offer many spiritual blessings. Accountability, fellowship, encouragement and study are only a few. Lastly, social witness allows the Christian family to move beyond themselves and reach out to meet the needs of those in society who are hurting and in need.

Many of these elements have been lost in our churches and culture. If we are to be the church that God has called us to be, we should draw from the witness of John Wesley and take up his missionary charge to meet the needs of the whole person in our society. Let us do good to the souls of others, "especially to those of the household of faith" (see Galatians 6:10).

REFLECTION QUESTIONS

1. What element of John Wesley's ministry appeals most to you? Explain why.

2. What elements of Wesley's ministry do you think need to be recovered in the church today? Why and how?

3. What can the modern Christian church gain from rediscovering John Wesley's ministry and practice?

4. Are there any areas of Wesley's ministry you don't agree with or think could be or have been improved upon?

Endnotes

[1] John Wesley, *Works*, 5:303-4.

[2] John Telford, ed., *The Letters of John Wesley* (London: Epworth, 1960) 332-70.

[3] *Works*, 1:185.

[4] Curnock, Nehemiah. *The Journals of the Rev. John Wesley* (London: Epworth, 1938) 8:110.

[5] Francis Asbury, *The Journal and Letters of Francis Asbury* (Nashville: Abingdon, 1958) 2:787, cited in Robert E. Coleman, *"Nothing to Do but to Save Souls." John Wesley's Charge to His Preachers* (Grand Rapids, MI: Francis Asbury, 1990).

[6] *Works*, 1:416.

[7] *Works*, 3:144.

[8] Albert Outler, *John Wesley* (New York: Oxford, 1964) 178.

[9] Outler, 181.

[10] Outler, 178.

[11] *Works*, 11:433.

[12] Outler, 86.

[13] Outler, 179.

[14] Bready J. Wesley, *England: Before and After Wesley* (London: Hodder and Stoughton, n.d.) 238.

[15] Wesley, *Poetical Works*, I:IX-XXII, cited in D. Michael Henderson, *John Wesley's Class Meeting: A Model for Making Disciples* (Nappanee, IN: Evangel Publishing, 1997) 86.

chapter four

Wesley's Leaders

We cannot understand the Methodist revival without looking at the leaders of the Movement. John Wesley had the ability to gather great men and women around him who would stand behind his cause and become leaders of the Methodist revival. He was an amazing leader who had a God-given talent for recognizing the best in people and developing the leadership qualities in others. Among the early Methodists, several key personalities emerged to become great leaders of the Movement. These leaders helped Wesley spread the cause of Methodism throughout the British Isles, into North America, and eventually throughout the world. Although each one was different, they all helped contribute in their own special way to the spread of Methodism.

Charles Wesley

John's brother, Charles Wesley, was a lifelong companion in ministry and a coleader in the Methodist Movement. In the 1720s, Charles was the first "Methodist" at Oxford College. Later, in 1729, John became the leader of the Oxford Methodists. Charles Wesley was a gifted songwriter and a preacher in his own right. He was the author of over 500 hymns, which can be found in the *Collection of Hymns for the Use of the People Called Methodist*. Some of these beloved hymns were "Hark! The Herald Angels Sing," "Love Divine," "Jesus, Lover of My Soul" and "O for a Thousand Tongues."

From the very beginning they seemed destined to work together in ministry. They were together in the early formation of Methodism. Both were ordained in the Church of England around the same time. In 1735, they traveled together to be missionaries in Georgia, and when they returned to England, both experienced a similar heartwarming experience. Throughout the years of the Methodist revival, John continually relied on Charles for personal counsel and assistance. Although they were together much of their lives, John and Charles did not always agree on everything. Sometimes they disagreed on the practice of lay preaching, the ordination of lay ministers, the relation of Methodism to the Church of England, and occasionally over doctrine. Although they did not always see eye to eye, their love and affection for one another is clearly evident. In 1788, shortly after Charles' death, John broke down in tears while singing the lyrics to one of Charles' hymns, "My companion before me is gone."

John Fletcher

John Fletcher was one of the most beloved disciples of John Wesley. Fletcher was ordained as a priest in the Church of England in March 1757, and became vicar of Madeley in 1760. Fletcher was a brilliant scholar and a man of tremendous piety. He served three years as the president of Trevecca College, but resigned over doctrinal differences with the Calvinist Methodist. He is well known for his *Checks to Antinomianism*, which defended Wesley's theology against the Calvinist and became standard reading for early Methodists in the British Isles and North America.

Wesley was so impressed with Fletcher that he designated him to be his chosen successor. Fletcher, however, never became an itinerant preacher; rather he chose to remain a parish vicar. Although he was not a traveling preacher, he served the Movement most through his written defense of Wesley's doctrine of Christian perfection. He was married to Mary Bosanquet, an important Methodist woman preacher. Together they ministered to their flock at Madeley. Although Fletcher was Wesley's chosen successor, he died on August 14, 1785, six years before Wesley. Despite being a marvelous theologian, he lived and died caring for his congregation.

Adam Clarke

Adam Clarke was converted to Methodism in 1778 under the preaching of Thomas Barber. He was a teenager when he dedicated his life to God. Under Wesley's invitation, he trained for the ministry. He was among some of the earliest lay preachers to be ordained by Wesley. He quickly became one of the most prominent leaders of the Methodist Movement. He was a gifted leader and preacher, a competent Biblical scholar and a prolific writer. Although he had no formal education, he was fluent in at least 20 languages including Greek, Latin, Hebrew, Samaritan, Syriac, Arabic, Persian and Coptic.

It is estimated that he preached some 15,000 sermons during his lifetime. He preached for the masses and wrote for the learned. He wrote an eight-volume *Commentary on the Holy Scriptures*, which became required reading for Methodist clergy, even long after his death. He was loved among the Methodist preachers and served an impressive three terms as president of the Wesleyan Conference. His writings contributed to the spread of the Wesleys' doctrine of holiness. He died in 1832 of cholera, but left a wonderful legacy.

Thomas Coke

Dr. Thomas Coke was a passionate soulwinner who was converted to Methodism in 1772, two years after being ordained in the Church of England. Within only a year, his Anglican parishioners dismissed him because he had begun to preach like a Methodist. He then joined the Methodist Movement full-time and soon became one of Wesley's most able leaders and closest associates. Wesley designated him as a co-superintendent with Francis Asbury to set the American Methodist Church in order in 1784, but he would not stay long.

He only remained in America for a few years before setting his eyes on the mission field. In 1789, he was appointed head of the Irish Conference. The following years of his life were dedicated to supporting and promoting world missions. Toward the end of his life he longed to take the gospel to India. He said, "I am dead to Europe and alive for India." He finally persuaded the Methodists to allow him to go to Ceylon, India. Then in 1814, he died in prayer on the way to India. Dr. Coke was one of Wesley's greatest leaders who left a missionary legacy for the church.

Francis Asbury

The amazing growth of Methodism in America after the Revolutionary War was partly due to the ministry of Francis Asbury. He was sent by John Wesley to promote Methodism in the Colonies and soon became the leader of the American movement. Although English-born, he won the hearts and souls of the American people. America was truly his parish. Throughout his 45-year ministry in America, he traveled nearly 300,000 miles on horseback, preached about 16,500 sermons and ordained more than 4,000 preachers.

Asbury was a man of great piety and learning, a tireless leader who devoted his entire life to the call of Christ in America. Many people said he was a great man of prayer. Through his constant travels and ministry endeavors, he still found time to pray. He would often rise at 4 in the morning and spend around two hours in prayer and meditation every day. In addition, he prayed seven times a day.

Although he dropped out of school before he was 12, he taught himself to read Latin, Greek and Hebrew. He also founded five schools and promoted Sunday schools, which taught children reading and writing. He made it a habit to rise before 5 a.m. for the study of Scripture. He was widely read on various subjects of his day. He could be found reading a book while riding horseback, as was the practice of many of the circuit riders. It has been said that he was one of the most well-informed men of his day and could converse on any subject.

He was a master at organizational leadership. He created what is called a "district," which was a circuit of churches that would be served by a preacher called a "circuit rider." The circuit rider would travel from church to church to preach and minister. These preachers braved the rigors of the wild frontier, which included Indian attacks and illness. Many of them did not live past the age of 30. Although Asbury was plagued by bad health all of his life, he continued to travel, even if it meant being tied to his saddle to keep from falling from his horse. It is said that the wolves would follow him to wait on him to die. Francis Asbury is arguably one of the greatest leaders the Methodist church has ever known. He is the Great American Bishop.

Women Preachers

A discussion on Wesley's leaders would be void without mentioning several key women who became leaders in the Methodist revival. Wesley and early Methodism were ahead of their time in recognizing the rights of women and allowing them to participate in Christian ministry. Women served God at various levels in the Methodist Movement. Most of the class and band leaders were, in fact, women. These women were engaged in preaching and leading souls to Christ. Wesley took notice that God was indeed using them in this manner. Women such as Sarah Crosby, Mary Bosanquet, Hannah Harrison, Grace Murray and Hester Ann Roe Rogers were among the women lay ministers of Methodism. These women were also examples of piety, learning and leadership.

Mary Bosanquet, the wife of John Fletcher, became Methodism's first woman preacher who was also a lay theologian of sorts. She wrote a letter to John Wesley, defending the rights of women to preach the gospel. In it she argued that the Bible contained many accounts of women who were called of God to minister. As a result, Wesley recognized the extraordinary call of God on certain women to preach. In response to Mary Bosanquet's letter, he wrote the following:

> I think that the strength of the cause rests thereon your having an *extraordinary* call. So I am persuaded has every one of our lay preachers; otherwise I could not countenance his preaching at all. It is plain to me that the whole work of God termed *Methodism* is an *extraordinary dispensation* of His providence. Therefore I do not wonder if several things occur therein which do not fall under the ordinary rules of discipline.[1]

In 1787, despite opposition by certain male preachers, Wesley officially authorized Sarah Mallet to preach as long as she would keep Methodist doctrine and discipline. This was a bold stride toward full recognition of women as ministers, which would not take full fruition until long after Wesley's death. Wesley's views on women in ministry were revolutionary to his day. He believed women had equal rights. In a sermon titled "On Visiting the Sick," he addressed the equal rights of women:

> Let all you that have in your power assert the right which the God of nature has given you. Yield not to that bondage any longer! You, as well as men, are rational creatures. You, like them, were made in the image of God; you are equally candidates for immortality; you too are called of God, as you have time, to "do good unto all men."[2]

Lessons for Today

Part of Wesley's genius was his ability to select, train and gather leaders around him who became extensions of his own personal vision. The rapid and miraculous growth of Methodism would not have been possible without the endeavors and self-sacrifice of these early Methodist leaders. They gave their whole lives for the cause of Christ and to the spread of Methodism. Many of them put their lives in harm's way to assure that Methodism would continue to grow. They had grit and determination, which has not been seen since the persecutions of the early church.

Thomas Paine said, "What we obtain too cheap, we esteem too lightly." Therefore, it can be said that Methodism was born with a great price—the lives of great men and women. Among them were prominent women of devotion who served as leaders of class meetings. They visited the sick and preached the gospel. Together these men and women helped Methodism become one of the fastest-growing movements the world has ever known.

REFLECTION QUESTIONS

1. What is your general impression of the leaders of early Methodism?

2. Among the various leaders of early Methodism, who stands out the most to you? Please explain why.

3. What are some general characteristics that all Christian leaders, both past and present, seem to have in common?

4. What is your personal impression and opinion of women in ministry? Was Wesley justified in allowing them to minister?

5. Can you see ways in which the influence of these leaders has influenced your denomination and church?

Endnotes

[1] John Telford, ed. *The Letters of the Rev. John Wesley*, 8 vols (London: Epworth, 1931) 5:257.

[2] John Wesley, *Works*, 7:126

chapter five

The Later Years

There is a saying that wine gets better with age. The same could be said of John Wesley, because his later years were as productive—if not more so—than his earlier years as the leader of the Methodist revival. The mark of true leaders is the ability to prepare their organization to outlast themselves. Wesley not only did this, but he also worked hard to create an organizational structure and a leadership team that would ensure Methodism would continue to thrive long after his death. Rather than being a time of relenting, his final years were spent working hard to consolidate the Movement. Several major developments in the later years of his life assured him that his Movement would continue beyond his days.

New Chapel

By the late 1770s, the Foundry had begun to wear down and become too small for the Methodists in London. There was a growing need to find permanent headquarters for Methodism. Out of necessity, Wesley built the New Chapel in City Road, which became the new headquarters of Methodism. In April 1777, he laid the foundation for the chapel and in 1778 Samuel Tooth, a class leader and local preacher, built it. It was not only a preaching house, but it was also the first Methodist chapel to include an altar and Communion rail. The chapel seated about 1,500 people and provided a home for Wesley and the preachers of the chapel, their families and servants. During the laying of the foundation, he preached a sermon that highlighted the rise of Methodism and connected the Movement to the primitive religion of the Bible. Some have called the chapel the "Mother of World Methodism" because it became the center for Methodist leadership, influence and activities through-out the world.

Deed of Declaration

In 1778, Wesley made provision for a stable governmental system that would assure that Methodism would remain intact after his death. On February 28, 1787, he initiated the Deed of Declaration, which gave legal rights to the preachers of the Methodist Conference. The Deed listed 100 preachers by name and gave them the right to meet once a year to elect a president and a secretary, appoint preachers to circuits, admit candidates for ministry, and conduct general business for the Methodist Conference. The annual conference was also an opportunity for the preachers to be heard, to have fellowship with one another, and to share their triumphs and trials from the previous year.

Some of the preachers who were not among the initial 100 were offended because they had not been included. Wesley argued that all of the preachers could not attend because that would have left vacancies in many of the circuits. After Wesley's death, the Conference extended the privileges of the Deed of Declaration to all preachers in full fellowship with the Conference. The Deed of Declaration solidified the Methodist Movement by legally giving the power of the church to the preachers. Thus, today the Methodist Conference still meets annually in much the same way it did in Wesley's day.

Consolidation of American Methodism

Due to the fact that lay ministers could not administer the sacraments, Methodists in America were dependent on the Anglican clergy to baptize their children and serve the Lord's Supper. Certain lay ministers, like Strawbridge, felt the necessity to administer the sacraments even though they were not ordained. Because of growing pressure to provide proper spiritual care for his flock in America, Wesley reluctantly decided to ordain lay preachers for the work in America.

On September 18, 1784, Wesley ordained Richard Whatcoat and Thomas Vasey, and dedicated Thomas Coke, an Anglican priest. Coke and the other two were sent to the Colonies with instructions to organize the American Methodist Church and ordain ministers. Directions were given to install Coke and Asbury as superintendents of the new church. They also brought with them a prayer book based on the Anglican liturgy, *The Sunday Service of the Methodists in North America,* and *A Collection of Psalms and Hymns for the Lord's Day.* The Sunday service included a set of 24 doctrinal statements called the *Articles of Religion,* which were simplified from the Anglican 39 *Articles of Religion.*

On December 24, 1784, American Methodists held the now famous Christmas Conference, at the Lovely Lane Chapel in Baltimore, Maryland, to organize the new church. The Methodist Episcopal Church in America was the newly adopted name, and Asbury and Coke were unanimously reelected superintendents by the preachers. Several ministers received ordination, which permitted them to administer the sacraments. The newly formed church added an article at the Christmas Conference that recognized the United States as a sovereign and independent nation. The conference also approved a motion that prohibited Methodists from participating in slave trade. This would later cause division in the church. They added John Wesley's Standard Sermons and his *Notes Upon the New Testament* as additional doctrinal standards.

The Christmas Conference, thought to be the cradle of American Methodism, marked the official organization of the American Methodist Church, which today has numerous Methodist denominations. The conference also marked the beginning of the newly formed church's doctrinal standards and discipline, which continue to be an important guide for American Methodists today. At the time of the conference, American Methodism had a few hundred members and about 80 preachers. Under Asbury's leadership, Methodism grew to 200,000 strong with over 4,000 preachers.

Wesley had accomplished many of his goals for the Movement:

- He consolidated both the British and American Methodists by giving them the power to continue after his death.

- He saw his Movement spread throughout the British Isles and North America in a relatively short period of time.
- He saw hundreds of thousands of souls come to Christ as a result of his ministry endeavors.
- He created a class meeting system that would ensure his followers would continue to grow in the faith.
- He founded several educational institutions.
- He left his followers his written works, which were to serve as a basis for the doctrine and discipline of his Movement. He was the father of Methodism all the way to the end.

"God With Us"

Toward the end of his life, Wesley began to lose many of his close associates. John Fletcher died in 1785 and his brother Charles died in 1788. Despite the painful losses, Wesley was determined to be busy to the very end. In fact, he said that he did not want to live to be useless. He remained very active in his old age, writing numerous sermons and letters, and publishing the *Arminian Magazine* until his death. He continued to travel, preach and oversee the Methodist Movement. The following quote gives a picture of the keen mind and wit that Wesley still possessed at age 85:

> I this day enter on my eighty-fifth year. And what cause have I to praise God, as for a thousand spiritual blessings, so for bodily blessings also! How little have I suffered yet, by the rush of numerous years! It is true, I am not so agile as I was in times past: I do not run or walk so fast as I did. My sight is a little decayed. My left eye

is grown dim, and hardly serves me to read. . . .
I find likewise some decay in my memory, with
regard to names and things lately past; but not at
all with regard to what I have read or heard
twenty, forty, or sixty years ago.[1]

He continued to preach and travel to the very end of his life. Although he became quite sickly, he preached several sermons in February of 1791. He preached his last sermon to a small group at Leatherhead on "Seek ye the Lord while he may be found, call ye upon him while he is near" (Isaiah 55:6). The next day he penned his last letter to William Wilberforce, exhorting him to remain steadfast in his endeavors against slavery. His mind remained as sharp as it ever was. Then, toward the end of February 1791, Wesley became very ill. He returned to City Road to prepare for his death. Both friends and family were called to say their last good-byes to the weary saint.

During his last night, he faintly whispered, "I'll praise, I'll praise." Then in what would be his last words he said, "The best of all is God is with us." The next morning on March 2, 1791, he passed into eternity to be with the Lord at the age of 88. Wesley was laid to rest in the cemetery at his chapel at City Road in London. Nearly 10,000 people came out to see his funeral. The following inscription is on the marble tablet placed in the chapel at City Road:

Sacred to the Memory
Of the Reverend John Wesley, M.A.,
Sometime Fellow of Lincoln College, Oxford;
A Man in Learning and sincere Piety
Scarcely inferior to any;

In Zeal, Ministerial Labours, and extensive
Usefulness,
Superior, perhaps to all Men,
Since the days of St. Paul.

Regardless of Fatigue, personal danger, and
Disgrace,
He went out into the highways and the hedges
Calling Sinners to Repentance,
And publishing the Gospel of Peace.
He was the founder of the Methodist Societies,
And the chief Promoter and Patron
Of the Plan of Itinerant preaching,
Which He extended through Great Britain and
Ireland,
The West Indies and America,
With unexampled Success.
He was born the 17th of June, 1703;
And died the 2nd of March, 1791,
In Sure and certain hope of Eternal Life,
Through the Atonement and Mediation of a
Crucified Savior.

Lessons for Today

The later years of John Wesley's life were as productive as his earlier years. The true test of a leader is not how you start the race, but how you finish it. It can truly be said that Wesley finished well. In his final years, he worked hard to strengthen and consolidate the great advances of the Methodist revival. He created an organizational structure and a leadership team that would last long after his death.

The mark of a great leader is the ability to ensure that his organization will outlive and outlast him. In fact, over 300 years after Wesley's death, his legacy is as strong as it ever was. We should ask ourselves, "What will I leave to the world when I die?"

I believe that Wesley would want us to help make the world a better place. He left the following challenge to the church: "It matters not how long we live, but how well."

REFLECTION QUESTIONS

1. In what ways has the life of John Wesley inspired or encouraged your Christian faith?

2. In what ways does John Wesley's influence still remain in the church today?

3. What interesting fact did you learn about Wesley's followers?

4. Did you think that Wesley was justified in organizing the Methodist Church in America, despite his allegiance to the Anglican Church? Explain.

5. Among the various events of Wesley's life, which one do you think was the most significant? Have you experienced similar events?

6. Do you think the church needs to become more aware of John Wesley's life and ministry? Why or why not? In what ways do you think the church could benefit from learning more about John Wesley?

7. How can a study of one of the most influential Christian leaders of all time impact your life? What do you expect to gain from such a study?

Endnotes

[1] John Wesley, *The Works of*, 5:39.

part two

John Wesley's
Message

* * * * * * *

LOVE DIVINE

Love divine, all loves excelling,
Joy of heaven, to earth come down!
Fix in us Thy humble dwelling,
All Thy faithful mercies crown;
Jesus, Thou art all compassion,
Pure, unbounded love Thou art;
Visit us with Thy salvation,
Enter every trembling heart.

Come, Almighty to deliver,
Let us all Thy life receive;
Suddenly return, and never,
Nevermore, Thy temples leave;
Thee we would be always blessing,
Serve Thee as Thy hosts above,
Pray, and praise Thee without ceasing,
Glory in Thy perfect love.

Finish then Thy new creation,
Pure and spotless let us be;
Let us see Thy great salvation,
Perfectly restored in Thee;
Changed from glory into glory,
Till in heaven we take our place,
Till we cast our crowns before Thee,
Lost in wonder, love, and praise!

—Charles Wesley

chapter six

Major Themes in Wesley's Message

This chapter examines several of the main themes in John Wesley's practical theology.

> "I design plain truth for plain people: Therefore, of set purpose, I abstain from all nice and philosophical speculations; from all perplexed and intricate reasonings; and, as far as possible, from even the show of learning, unless in sometimes citing the original Scriptures."[1]

A concern for the process of salvation can be seen throughout the works of John Wesley. He sought to understand and explain authentic Christian experience in a way that people could understand. The way of salvation, which is sometimes called the order of salvation (*via salutis* or *ordo salutis*), refers to the process of salvation in the life of a believer. This process is made of specific distinct crisis events in the Christian's life, beginning with the prevenient grace of God. God is the author and finisher of the Christian faith. Each area of the order of salvation is a distinct work of the Spirit in the inward heart and soul of the human being. The process involves the justification, repentance, regeneration, assurance and sanctification of the believer. Each area of God's redemptive grace in the way of salvation will be further examined in this chapter.

Wesley's practical theology shows us the importance of the salvation process. Each major point of the order of salvation must be present in the lives of Christians to authentically be growing in the faith. The way of salvation was a special emphasis in John Wesley's theology. He wanted all of humanity to experience the life-transforming power of the gospel. Not only did he preach these marvelous truths, but he also shared them in his writings, hymns and journals for all people to read and reread. He tried to put them in the hands of every Methodist. While reading Wesley, one cannot help but encounter the very same truths he passionately speaks about.

PREVENIENT GRACE

The doctrine of original sin teaches that humanity is totally deprived and lost since the fall of Adam. At first glance such a doctrine appears hopeless until you begin to understand the teaching of *prevenient grace*. Wesley understood prevenient grace as the grace of God that operates before conversion. *Prevenient* (*pre-venio*) literally means "comes before." The Holy Spirit is actively working in people's lives to awaken their heart, mind and soul to the need of salvation. It is only then a person can truly accept the grace of God. Wesley said, "God worketh in you; therefore, you can work; otherwise, it would be impossible. If he did not work, it would be impossible for you to work out your own salvation."[2]

This grace creates in us an awareness of our sinfulness before God. Wesley saw the need for lost humanity to have divine assistance in spiritual matters. He knew that human freedom alone could not bring about the desire, nor the strength, to accept God's free offer of salvation.

> Allowing that all souls of men are dead in sin by nature, this excuses none, seeing there is no man that is in a state of mere nature. There is no man, unless he has quenched the Spirit, that is wholly void of the grace of God. No man living is entirely destitute of what is vulgarly called "natural conscience." But this is not natural: it is more properly termed "preventing grace." Every man has a greater or less measure of this, which waiteth not for the call of man."[3]

Wesley was not trying to say that humans have a good nature; rather, he was saying that the grace of God was working in them, allowing them to turn to God in the first place. You might call this a divine invitation in which the Holy Spirit invites us to receive God's free gift of salvation, but we must accept or decline this offer. The prevenient grace of God works in us to convict us of sin. It could be said that it prepares people for salvation by awakening them to their own sinfulness and their need for God. God's grace frees us to understand and accept God's free offer of forgiveness and reconciliation, and moves us to repentance and regeneration. The Spirit works as a guide at this point to lead us to Jesus Christ.

Universal Grace

Because of God's prevenient grace, all of humanity has the potential to receive salvation. Indeed, Wesley felt that this grace was free for all. He said, "There is no man, unless he has quenched the Spirit, that is wholly void of the grace of God. No man living is entirely destitute of what is vulgarly called 'natural conscience.' But this is not natural; it is more properly termed "preventing grace."[4]

It is the Holy Spirit who works in the hearts of men and women to accept His free salvation. With Wesley, we can affirm that God's salvation is "free in all, free for all."[5] Wesley's universal vision of the work of the Holy Spirit included people in every country and in every part of the world. There can be no doubt that Wesley "believed that God's Spirit was at work everywhere in the world extending God's prevenient graciousness among all peoples."[6] The Spirit offers Christ's salvation to all the people of the world, regardless of their nationality, socioeconomic background, ethnicity or gender.

JUSTIFICATION

Justification is a judicial act of God in which God remits the sins of the believer and declares him to be in a position of righteousness before God.[7]   Here John Wesley follows closely to his Reformation heritage on the doctrine of justification. In his sermon on "Justification by Faith," Wesley points out that it is by the merits of Christ that we receive justification, which is the forgiveness of sins. We are saved from the guilt of sin and restored to the favor of God. *Justification* is an unmerited act of God where believers are forgiven of their sins and where the process of sanctification begins.

It is important not to confuse justification with regeneration or sanctification, as some have done. Wesley clearly distinguished between the two. He said that the doctrine of justification is what God does for us and regeneration is the actual change God begins to work in us.[8] There is an important difference. *Justification* is the point where we are forgiven from our sins and brought back into a right relationship with God through the merit of Jesus Christ. He further said that justification is not actually being made just and righteous—this is sanctification.[9] The Scriptural concept of justification is the forgiveness of sins—nothing more, nothing less. The change begins with regeneration, or the new birth.

Repentance

We must also make a distinction between repentance and justification. Wesley said repentance is "conviction of sin, producing real desires and sincere resolutions of amendment."[10] *Repentance* is an act of a man or woman, while *justification* is an act of God. Wesley differed from the Reformed thinkers on the time when these occur. Wesley believed that repentance preceded justifying faith, while the Reformers believed that it followed. He said, "We must repent before we can believe."[11]

Kenneth Collins says that "for Wesley, whenever justification is present, repentance necessarily precedes. However, where repentance is present, justification does not immediately and necessarily follow."[12] Therefore, repentance must always come before justification of a believer and not vice versa.

By Faith

Justification by faith was the hallmark of the Protestant Reformation. John Wesley did not stray at all from his Anglican tradition on this issue. He believed that when a person's faith was fused with the prevenient grace of God, it would result in their justification. In his sermon "The Lord Our Righteousness," he makes this statement:

> That we are justified by faith alone is spoken to take away clearly all merits of our works, and wholly to ascribe the merit and deserving of our justification to Christ alone. Our justification comes freely of the mercy of God . . . Christ therefore is now the righteousness of all them that truly believe in him.[13]

There is no true justification without faith. Faith is the necessary condition for our justification.[14] Our faith in Christ frees us from having to depend on works of the law or the flesh for salvation. Wesley also believed that good works would naturally follow justification by faith.

> All truly *good works* (to use the words of our church) *follow after justification*; and they are therefore "good and acceptable to God in Christ," because they "spring out of a true and living faith."[15]

As we can see, true justification will be preceded by repentance and followed by the fruit of faith, which is good works. This does not imply that salvation is based on works, rather that our faith will result in good works.

NEW BIRTH

Wesley saw the tremendous need for humanity to experience the life-transforming power of the new birth we find in John 3:7: "Ye must be born again." Therefore, the new birth is at the heart of John Wesley's message and ministry. He used the terms *new birth*, *born again*, and *regeneration* interchangeably. The word *regeneration* literally means "rebirth." It is a spiritual birth, whereby we are born again by the Spirit in a moment. *Regeneration* is a spiritual transformation whereby the Holy Spirit takes us from death unto life. Wesley used the analogy of natural birth and growth to parallel the new birth and sanctification.

> A child is born of a woman in a moment. Afterwards he gradually and slowly grows till he attains the stature of a man. In like manner a child is born of God in a short time, if not a moment. But it is by slow degrees that he afterward grows up to the measure of the full stature of Christ.[16]

The new birth is a crisis experience that happens instantaneously. There may be pain and travail that precede birth, but when the proper time comes, birth happens in a moment. So it is when we are born again. In a moment, we are changed and given a new life in Christ. In the words of the apostle Paul, "If any man be in Christ, he is a new creature: old things are passed away; behold, all things are become new" (2 Corinthians 5:17).

Real Change

A glorious change takes place in believers' hearts when they receive Christ into their life by faith. It is both a real and a relative change where they are inwardly renewed by the power of God.[17]

According to Wesley . . .

> [The new birth] is a great change that God works
> in our soul when he brings it into life; when he
> raises it from the death of sin into the life of right-
> eousness. It is the change wrought in the whole
> soul by the almighty Spirit of God when it is cre-
> ated anew in Christ Jesus, when it is renewed
> after the image of God, in righteousness and true
> holiness, when the love of the world is changed
> into the love of God, pride into humility, passion
> into meekness; hatred, envy, malice, into sincere,
> tender, disinterested love for all mankind.[18]

This great change entails an exchange of the things of the world for the things of God. It is a total transformation, in which the new believer is literally made a new creature. A believer is changed inwardly. The Spirit of God is the agent of regeneration that works to bring about this change in a person's heart.

Christianity is essentially an inward religion of the heart. The heart and soul of a person is the place where the Holy Spirit brings about a "real and relative change" in the believer. This change is also a restoration of the image of God. When Adam fell, the Bible says that all fell into sin. The original image of God was marred from that time until Christ. Jesus Christ is the Second Adam, who has made a way through the Spirit to restore the image of God in the hearts, minds and souls of born-again believers through salvation.

Marks of the New Birth

In his sermon on the "Marks of the New Birth," Wesley establishes that there are distinguishable marks and visible fruits of the new birth. He summarized the Scriptural marks of those who are born of God as faith, hope and love.

1. The first mark of the new birth is faith. An immediate and constant fruit of faith is power over sin. It is a faith that frees and a faith that flees from sin. Another fruit of faith is peace, which is promised so often in Scripture (Romans 5:1; John 14:27; 16:33).

2. A second mark of the new birth is hope. *Hope* is a full assurance of faith of salvation, which is given by the Spirit who bears witness with our spirit that we are children of God.

3. The third mark of the new birth is the greatest of all—love. *Love* is the supreme goal of the Christian faith, summed up by loving the Lord with all of your heart, soul and mind, and loving your neighbor as yourself (Matthew 22:37-39).

4. Finally, the change that takes place in the lives of believers when they are born again will manifest itself with spiritual fruit unto holiness. The change that occurs at the new birth prepares the Christian for ongoing sanctification and growth in grace.

ASSURANCE

A group called the *Moravians* helped John Wesley realize the need for the experience of Christian assurance. Over time, he began to realize he did not have the inner "witness of the Spirit" that he was a child of God. This led him to search the Scriptures and dialogue with others who testified of having Christian assurance. The stage was set for Wesley's much-debated "Aldersgate" experience. Then on May 24, 1738, John Wesley testified, "I felt my heart strangely warmed. I felt I did trust in Christ, Christ alone for salvation; and an assurance was given me that he had taken away my sins, even mine, and saved me from the law of sin and death."[19]

The Witness of the Spirit

The Holy Spirit plays an important role in the assurance of the believer. "The Spirit itself beareth witness with our spirit, that we are the children of God" (Romans 8:16). Wesley used this scripture to give an explication of the work the Spirit does in His children. The Spirit who inspired the Scriptures continuously works to confirm the experiential truths found within its texts. In fact, Wesley believed that the witness of the Spirit confirmed what the Scriptures taught concerning experience. He said, "What the Scripture promises, I enjoy. Come and see what Christianity has done here; and acknowledge it is of God."[20]

In "The Witness of the Spirit" (1746), Wesley sought first to describe the connection between the "witness of the Spirit" and the witness of our spirit; and secondly, to distinguish it from the presumption of a natural mind. This was an attempt to answer the critics who opposed his doctrine of assurance (who charged him with enthusiasm), and to instruct his followers how to discern between the genuine witness of the Spirit and feelings to keep them from falling into enthusiasm.[21] A part of the problem was enthusiasts claimed to have the inner work of the Spirit without bearing the outward fruit of the Spirit.

The Witness of Our Spirit

In the "Witness of the Spirit," Wesley's focus was on the following:

> The testimony of the Spirit as an inward impression on the soul, whereby the Spirit of God directly witnesses to my spirit, that I am a child of God; that Jesus Christ hath loved, and given himself for

me; and that all my sins are blotted out, and I, even
I, am reconciled to God.[22]

The testimony of the Spirit must be an antecedent to
the testimony of our spirit. Wesley said, "We cannot
know his pardoning love to us, till his Spirit witnesses
it to our spirit."[23] The Spirit of God comes before the
testimony of our spirit, gives us the divine testimony
and allows our testimony to confirm it. The two witnesses work together in order to let us know that we
have become a child of God.

This testimony must have discernable features. He
describes the testimony of our spirit as "a conscious-
ness that we are inwardly conformed, by the Spirit of
God, to the image of his Son, and that we walk before
him in justice, mercy and truth, doing the things
which are pleasing in his sight."[24]

Marks of Assurance

The witness of the Spirit with our spirit demands an
ethical response to God. For Wesley, the doctrine of the
Spirit is never merely spiritual without an ethical
imperative, or vice versa.[25] There are several distinctive
ethical marks that distinguish true assurance from
false assurance:

1. Repentance, or conviction of sin, as constantly
going before the witness of pardon.

2. There will be a vast and mighty change "from
darkness to light," as well as "from the power of Satan
unto God."[26]

3. We keep His commandments. Wesley said, "A
true lover of God hastens to do his will on earth as it is
done in heaven."[27]

4. By the fruits of the Spirit, which He has wrought

in your spirit, you shall know the testimony of the Spirit of God. There are both immediate fruits (love, joy, peace) and outward fruits (doing good to all men; doing no evil, walking in the light).[28]

These distinguishing marks accompany the true testimony of the Spirit with the spirit of a believer and should become discernable to others. As the witness of the Spirit confirms the new birth, the Spirit confirms with our spirit that we are indeed children of God.

REFLECTION QUESTIONS

1. What elements of John Wesley's theology seem most appealing to you? Why?

2. Can you see ways in which Wesley's theology has influenced your particular church or denomination? Explain how.

3. What can we gain from looking at Wesley's theology today?

4. Are there elements of his theology you have never heard or seen before?

5. Are there ways in which his theology challenges you to live a better Christian life? Explain how.

Endnotes

[1] John Wesley, *Works*, Preface to the Sermons, 5:3.

[2] *Works*, 6:511.

[3] *Works*, 6:511.

[4] *Works*, 6:511.

[5] *Works*, 7:373.

[6] Theodore Runyon, *The New Creation: John Wesley's Theology Today* (Nashville: Abingdon, 1998) 33.

[7] R. Hollis Gause, *Living in the Spirit: The Way of Salvation* (Cleveland, TN: Pathway, 1980) 10.

[8] *Works*, 5:56.

[9] *Works*, 8:47.

[10] *Works*, 5:241, cited in Steve Harper, *John Wesley's Message for Today* (Grand Rapids: Zondervan, 1983) 53.

[11] Kenneth Collins, *The Scriptural Way of Salvation* (Nashville: Abingdon, 1997) 73.

[12] *Works*, 5:239.

[13] *Works*, 5:53-64.

[14] *Works*, 5:59.

[15] *Works*, 6:75.

[16] Albert Outler, *John Wesley* (New York: Oxford, 1964) 274.

[17] *Works*, 6:71.

[18] *Works*, 1:103.

[19] *Works*, 10:79.

[20] This was an argument that was important enough for him to write a second discourse by the same title in 1767, over 20 years later. See also "The Witness of Our Own Spirit" (1746) and "The Nature of Enthusiasm" (1750).

[22] *Works*, 5:115.

[23] *Works*, 5:115.

[24] *-Works*, 5:115.

[25] Outler, "A Focus on the Holy Spirit: Spirit and Spirituality in John Wesley," *Quarterly Review*, 1988: 168.

[26] *Works*, 5:118.

[27] *Works*, 5:120.

[28] *Works*, 5:122.

chapter seven

Wesley and the Means of Grace

When reading the works of John Wesley, we see that he spent a great deal of time and energy promoting means of grace. He saw the need for Christians to have means that would assist them in their growth in grace. These means were vital to his own personal growth and development as a Christian.

As the evangelical revival swept throughout England and North America, he saw that many fell away if they had no means of spiritual formation to assist them in their growth. He expected all who continued to evidence their desire for salvation to attend on all the ordinances of God. He placed special emphasis on spiritual formation through the means of grace, where God provides sustaining grace for believers.

The *means of grace* are ways that God chooses at various times to nourish, enrich and sanctify Christians throughout the process of their lifetime. Wesley believed the means of grace were "outward sign, words or actions, ordained of God, and appointed for this end, to be the ordinary channels whereby He might convey to men, preventing, justifying or sanctifying grace."[1]

Another key to understanding the means of grace is, "If separate from the Spirit of God, [grace] cannot profit at all, cannot conduce in any degree, either to the knowledge or love of God."[2] So without the accompanied presence of the Holy Spirit, the means of grace are meaningless.

The means of grace are numerous; however, Wesley does emphasize the following three as being the "chief" means in his sermon on the means of grace:

> The chief of these means are prayer, whether in secret or with the great congregation; searching the Scriptures (which implies reading, hearing, and meditating thereon); and receiving the Lord's Supper, eating bread and drinking wine in remembrance of Him: And these we believe to be ordained of God, as the ordinary channels of conveying his grace to the souls of men."[3]

Wesley listed the following means in his rules for bands Societies, 1738:

1. To be at church, and at the Lord's Table, every week, and at every public meeting of the bands.

2. To attend the ministry of the Word every morning, unless distance, business, or sickness, prevent.

3. To use private prayer every day, and family prayer if you are the head of a family.

4. To read the Scriptures, and meditate thereon, at every vacant hour.

5. To observe as days of fasting or abstinence all Fridays of the year.

Although there are many means of grace, we will look briefly at the following means of grace: prayer, fasting, searching the Scriptures, the Lord's Supper and public worship.

Prayer

Wesley said that prayer was the "grand means of drawing near to God."[4] He listed prayer as one of the chief means of grace. Therefore, it can rightly be said of John Wesley that he was a man of prayer. He spent countless hours each day seeking the face of God in prayer. He would pray early in the morning, throughout the day, and late in the evening. He described a Methodist as one who "prays without ceasing" and whose "heart is ever lifted up to God, at all times and in all places."[5] Prayer is the best way we can encounter and commune with the living God.

He encouraged and practiced private, public and family prayers, believing that both private and corporate prayer were equally important. Corporate prayer took place within the context of a church and in the class meetings. This also took the form of written and liturgical prayers. He believed that praying written, formal prayers helped give structure to a person's prayer life. He used the Church of England's *Book of Common Prayer*, and even published his own prayer book for his followers to use in private and public prayer. In it, he included prayers for special days of the week, prayers for families and for children. He extended prayer to children, believing that they too could share in the privilege of prayer. He saw the importance for families to be engaged in prayer together.

Fasting

John Wesley saw fasting as a way to draw closer to God and to grow in holiness. He believed that fasting was a doctrinal practice that was grounded in the Bible. In his early ministry Wesley started fasting on

Wednesdays and Fridays. However, by 1738 Wesley seemed to advocate Fridays as the primary day to fast, a common custom of the Anglican Church. Fasting is one of the general ordinances Wesley prescribed for his followers. In his message on the Sermon on the Mount, Wesley says, "Fasting is a help to prayer; particularly when we set apart larger portions of time for private prayer." Fasting draws one nearer to God when it is done with right motivation, prayer and humility.

Holy Scriptures

Searching the Holy Scriptures is the second means of grace. Wesley's intense love for Scripture can be best described in his own words: "O give me that book! At any price, give me the book of God! I have it: Here is knowledge enough for me. Let me be *homo unius libri*."[6]

Wesley did not mean that other books were of no value to the Christian life, because he was an avid reader who often read on horseback and even compiled a *Christian Library* for his people to read. He believed that the Scriptures assisted believers on their journey of faith as they pressed on toward perfection. Regularly searching the Scriptures is absolutely necessary for the Christian faith to continue to grow. We should do this by reading, hearing and meditating on the Scriptures.

The Lord's Supper

Another important means of grace is receiving the Lord's Supper. While at Oxford, John and his brother, Charles, were accused of being "sacramentalist" because of their insistence on taking Communion regularly. It is said that he took the Lord's Supper at least once every four to five days, and he encouraged the Methodists to celebrate the Lord's Supper weekly. The grace of God is conveyed in the sacrament of the Lord's Supper through the "Real Presence" of Christ. He said, "Our bodies are strengthened by bread and wine, so are our souls by these tokens of the body and blood of Christ. This is the food of our souls: this gives strength to perform our duty and leads us on to perfection."[7] This grace is conveyed through the sacramental presence of the Holy Spirit that makes Christ's "Real Presence" available to the believer. We can see this demonstrated in the following hymn:

> Come, Holy Ghost, thine influence shed,
> And realize the sign;
> Thy life infuse into the bread,
> Thy power into the wine.
> Effectual let the tokens prove,
> And made, by heavenly art,
> Fit channels to convey thy love
> To every faithful heart.[8]

The Lord's Supper is a means of encounter with the living God. Therefore, we should follow Wesley's example and regularly receive the Lord's Supper.

Public Worship

Wesley saw the need for Christians to regularly attend public worship. This was an opportunity for Christians to express their love to God through corporate worship, praise and prayer. Methodists were encouraged to attend parish services of the Anglican Church. However, as Methodists were turned out of traditional churches, there was an increasing need to offer supplementary worship services to meet the needs of the people. Wesley eventually developed the *Sunday*

Service, which was based on the *Book of Common Prayer* to be used as a resource for American Methodists.

Wesley created two additional worship services called the Love Feast and the Covenant Service. The love feast was based on the early Christian agape meal. This was a service that he had adopted from the Moravians. These were services where Christians could praise the Lord in singing, testifying, prayer for one another, and fellowship by eating and drinking together. The Watch-Night Service was another important service in early Methodism. This began as a monthly celebration, but eventually became a New Year's Eve tradition. The purpose of the service was to provide an outlet for Christians to renew their covenant to God and to each other.

Lessons for Today

Wesley can show contemporary Christians the importance of using means of grace. God has given various things which can draw us closer to Him and perfect holiness in our lives. Many of these God-given means, lost to the church of today, desperately need to be recovered. Wesley reminds us of the importance of the Lord's Supper, prayer and fasting, reading the Scriptures, and public worship. Finally, John Wesley can be a guide for us as we continue to seek the Lord's will for our families. Family worship and prayer must be renewed if we are to have happy and healthy Christian homes.

REFLECTION QUESTIONS

1. What is your first impression of Wesley's emphasis on the means of grace?

2. Are there any means of grace that were not discussed that you feel are as important?

3. In what ways have you been changed or touched by the Lord when participating in one or more of the means of grace?

4. Can you see the need for Christians to recover the means of grace for today?

5. How could Wesley's means of grace be implemented in your local body of believers?

Endnotes

[1] *Works*, 5:187. See also Henry H. Knight III, *The Presence of God in the Christian Life: John Wesley and the Means of Grace* (Metuchen, N.J.: Scarecrow, 1971).

[2] *Works,* 5:188.

[3] *Works,* 5:187.

[4] See "Letters to Miss March" (29 Mar. 1760), *Letter* (Telford), 4:90. See also *Journal* (4 Sept. 1772), *Works,* 22:348. Cited in Maddox, *Responsible Grace.*

[5] *Works,* 8:343.

[6] *Works,* 5:3.

[7] Outler, *John Wesley,* 336.

[8] John and Charles Wesley, *A Collection of Hymns for the Use of the People Called Methodists,* ed. Franz Hildebrant and Oliver A. Beckerlegge, vol. 7 in the *Bicentennial Edition of the Works of John Wesley* (Nashville: Abingdon, 1989) Hymn 72.

chapter eight

Holiness of Heart and Life

Amidst the spiritual laxity and growing immorality of England and North America during the 18th century, John Wesley emerged as a champion of "Scriptural Christianity." One of Wesley's primary concerns was holiness of heart and life. Holiness and sanctification became a lifelong pursuit for John Wesley. Christian perfection was a hallmark of his message and ministry. One of his largest tracts was written on the subject of "Christian Perfection." He believed that God had chosen the Methodists to proclaim this Scriptural holiness.

In describing the Methodists, he called them "people who profess to pursue holiness of heart and life, inward and outward conformity in all things to the revealed will of God; who place religion in an uniform resemblance of the great object of it; in a steady imitation of Him they worship, in all His imitable perfections; more particularly, in justice, mercy, and truth, or universal love filling the heart, and governing the life."[1]

Holiness, then, can be described as "inward and outward conformity to the will of God." It is something that takes place both inwardly in the heart and manifests itself outwardly toward the world. Although most scholars are in agreement that holiness was a dominant theme of Wesley's theology, many of his descendants do not understand his doctrine of holiness. This chapter offers a brief overview of Wesley's concept of holiness.

HOLINESS OF HEART

Initial Sanctification

Wesley believed that from the time of our being born again, the gradual work of sanctification takes place.[2] This is commonly referred to as *initial sanctification*. *Sanctification* is salvation from the power of sin and restoration to the image of God. It is a process of being restored to the image of God, which begins at the new birth and gradually takes place over the lifetime of a believer. It is a real change in the heart, mind and soul of the believer. There is a difference between justification and initial sanctification, although they happen at the same time. He distinguished between the two in the following way:

> Afterwards we experience the proper Christian salvation; whereby, through grace, we are saved by faith; consisting of those two grand branches, justification and sanctification. By justification we are saved from the guilt of sin, and restored to the favor of God; by sanctification we are saved from the power and root of sin, and restored to the image of God.[3]

We can see how Wesley linked justification and sanctification, in that they occur at the same time, but they are not the same thing. Justification saves us from the guilt of sin, but sanctification saves us from the power of sin. It can be said that sanctification is the ethical counterpart of justification, but we must understand that there is also a gradual and instantaneous work of sanctification. The change begins at the new birth, but continues throughout a Christian's life.

Gradual Sanctification

Wesley spoke also about the progressive and gradual nature of sanctification. He said the new birth was the first point of sanctification, which may increase more and more unto the perfect day.[4] He believed that sanctification is a process of Christian growth where the Holy Spirit gradually sanctifies the hearts and minds of Christians. This means that Christians must be committed to going forward in faith, growing daily in Christ, and putting their sins behind them. He said that sanctification was both instantaneous and gradual and explained the difference:

> All experience, as well as Scripture, show this salvation to be both instantaneous and gradual. It begins in the moment we are justified in the holy, humble, gentle, patient love of God on man. It gradually increases from that moment, as "a grain of mustard seed," which, at first, is the least of all seeds, but afterwards puts forth large branches, and becomes a great tree; till, in another instant, the heart is cleansed from all sin, and filled with pure love to God and man. But even that love increases more and more, till we "grow up in all things into Him that is our head"; till we attain "the measure and fullness of Christ."[5]

As a newborn baby needs certain means to continue to grow and develop, so Christians need certain means to assist them in their growth. Wesley believed that there were things necessary to growth in sanctification, which he called works of piety and works of mercy. *Works of piety* included private, public and family prayer. It also included the Lord's Supper, hearing and reading the Scriptures, and fasting. The *works of mercy* are ministry to others. These included feeding the hungry; clothing the naked; entertaining the stranger; visiting those who are in prison, or sick, or afflicted; and contributing in any manner to the saving of souls. Although these are not necessary for salvation, he believed they are necessary for the process of sanctification.

Entire Sanctification

Although Wesley believed that sanctification was a process, he also believed in a second definite work of grace, in which a believer could experience entire sanctification. He said, "We wait for entire sanctification, for a full salvation from all our sins—from pride, self-will, anger, unbelief—or, as the apostle expresses it, 'go on unto perfection' [Hebrews 6:1]."[6] He taught that entire sanctification is received by faith, that it is given instantaneously, and that we are to expect it, not at death, but every moment. If the Bible said we could be perfect, then Christian perfection was attainable in this life. With Paul he could affirm, "The very God of peace sanctify you wholly" (1 Thessalonians 5:23).

Entire sanctification does not imply that believers will never sin again or that they are no longer liable to sin; rather, the one who is sanctified is freed from the power of sin in the present tense. This is no static event; the believer must continue to grow and "go on unto perfection."

The greatest emphasis Wesley placed on sanctification is that it is only possible through God's empowering presence. We are enabled to mortify the deeds of the flesh by the Spirit (see Romans 8:11). Wesley said that sanctification is what God works in us by His Spirit. Therefore, the Holy Spirit plays a unique role in the spiritual growth of a believer. Christian perfection is the gift of God and cannot be earned. It can only come from the sanctifying power and presence of the Holy Spirit. Entire sanctification is not possible through outward works alone (although they can be means of sanctifying grace), but can only be wrought by the sanctifying Spirit of God.

Perfect Love

Entire sanctification is also perfection in love. Wesley described Christian perfection as "loving God with all our hearts, mind, soul, and strength. This implies that no wrong temper, none contrary to love, remains in the soul and that all the thoughts, words and actions are governed by pure love."[7]

For Wesley, Christian perfection was perfection in love. In describing perfection in Hebrews 6:1, "go on unto perfection," he said, "The word has various senses: here it means perfect love. It is love excluding sin, love filling the heart, taking up the whole capacity of the soul. It is love 'rejoicing evermore, praying without ceasing, in everything giving thanks' [1Thessalonians 5:16-18]."[8] Holiness of heart is a perfect love for God, which manifests itself in a perfect love toward our neighbor and the world around us. Therefore, perfect love is the ultimate goal of the Christian life, which is attainable in this life.

What Perfection Is Not

There were many misunderstandings about Wesley's doctrine of Christian perfection. Critics criticized him and Methodists misunderstood his doctrine. Therefore, Wesley carefully distinguished between what Christian perfection is and is not.

In the year of 1764, upon review of the whole subject, I wrote down the sum of what I had observed in the following short propositions:

1. There is such thing as perfection; for it is again and again mentioned in Scripture.
2. It is not so early as justification; for justified persons are to "go unto perfection" (Hebrews 6:1).
3. It is not so late as death; for St. Paul speaks of living men that were perfect (Philippians 3:15).
4. It is not absolute. Absolute perfection belongs not to man, nor angels, but God alone.
5. It does not make a man infallible: None is infallible, while he remains in the body.
6. Is it sinless? It is not worthwhile to contend for a term. It is "salvation from sin."
7. It is "perfect love." (1 John 4:18). This is the essence of it; its properties, or inseparable fruits, are, rejoicing evermore, praying without ceasing, and in everything giving thanks (1 Thessalonians 5:16-18).
8. It is improvable. It is so far from lying in an indivisible point, from being incapable of increase that one perfected in love may grow in grace far swifter than he did before.
9. It is amissible, capable of being lost; of which we have numerous instances. But we were not lost thoroughly convinced of this, till five or six years ago.

10. It is constantly both preceded and followed by a gradual work.

11. But is in itself instantaneous or not? An instantaneous change has been wrought in some believers; none can deny this.[9]

Wesley wrote the preceding statements to simplify the complex doctrine of Christian perfection for both critics and Methodists alike. What we can learn from Wesley is the vital importance of holiness in the Christian life. Many simply opt for a view that says holiness is not possible, but as Wesley points out, Scripture emphasizes the promise of Christian perfection.

HOLINESS OF LIFE

Social Holiness

Wesley took holiness a step further and applied it to the social concerns of his day. He believed that Christianity is essentially a social religion, and to turn it into a solitary one is to destroy it.[10] He lampooned professors of religion who advised to cease from all outward action; wholly to withdraw from the world; to leave the body behind us; to abstract ourselves from all sensible things; to have no concern at all about outward religion, but to work all virtues in the will."[11]

Wesley was able to hold individual and social holiness in tension. He knew that the call to be separate was also a call to critically engage the world in love. Social holiness was one of Wesley's great contributions to Christianity via Methodism, the Holiness Movement of the 19th century, and more recently, the Pentecostal Movement.[12]

John Wesley believed that holiness was one of the main cornerstones of the Methodist Movement. He felt that a similar fate might befall the Methodists if they ever lost their doctrinal emphasis on holiness.

> I am not afraid that the people called Methodists should ever cease to exist either in Europe or America. But I am afraid, lest they should only exist as a dead sect, having the form of religion without the power. And this undoubtedly will be the case, unless they hold fast, both to the doctrine, spirit, and discipline with which they first set out.[13]

Lesson for Today

Holiness of heart and life produces passion for ministry within the context of the culture. The church's integration of holiness and ministry has radical social implications.[14]

Wesley speaks to us today about the importance of maintaining an integration of ministry, holiness and theology. John Wesley is a model for such integration. He said, "The beauty of holiness, of that inward man of the heart which is renewed after the image of God, cannot but strike every eye which God has opened, every enlightened understanding."[15] All will see our holiness of heart and life.

Holiness is both individual and outward; it is personal and social. The key to retaining our relevance as the people of God in the 21st century is by maintaining this tension. We should attempt to apply holiness to every area of our daily lives, both private and social. Only a radical commitment to loving the Lord and our

neighbor with all of our hearts will make a lasting difference in our society. Let us receive the challenge of
John Wesley "not to form any new sect; but to reform
the nation, particularly the Church; and to spread
scriptural holiness over the land."[16] Wesley reminds us
that we need to recover the vital doctrine of Christian
holiness in the day we live.

REFLECTION QUESTIONS

1. How can Wesley's concept of holiness make a difference in the world today?

2. How can his idea of holiness of heart and life become a greater reality in our lives? Explain.

3. Do you think the church needs to recover a proper idea of Christian holiness?

4. What ways has teaching on holiness and sanctification been lost in the church?

5. When was the last time you heard a sermon on this subject? Explain the content and conclusions of the message.

Endnotes

[1] *Works*, 8:352.

[2] Outler, *John Wesley*, 275.

[3] *Works*, 6:509.

[4] *Works*, 7:205.

[5] *Works*, 6:509.

[6] Outler, *John Wesley*, 275.

[7] Outler, *John Wesley*, 284.

[8] Outler, *John Wesley*, 275.

[9] *Works*, 11:441-442.

[10] *Works*, 5:294.

[11] *Works*, 5:295.

[12] See Donald Dayton, *Theological Roots of Pentecostalism* (New Jersey: Hendrickson, 1897); D. William Faupel, *The Everlasting Gospel: The Significance of Eschatology in the Development of Pentecostal Thought* (Sheffield, England: Sheffield Academic Press, 1996).

[13] *Works*, 13:258.

[14] Theodore Runyon, "Holiness as the Renewal of the Image of God in the Individual & Society," *Embodied Holiness* (Downers Grove, ILL: Intervarsity, 1999).

[15] *Works*, 5:295.

[16] *Works*, 8:299.

chapter nine

Wesley's Theological Method and the Holy Spirit

A key to understanding John Wesley's theology is to look at his theological method, which is Scripture, tradition, reason and experience—also called the Wesleyan Quadrilateral. When examining the Wesleyan Quadrilateral, it becomes apparent that each of the four religious sources is only effective through the work of the Holy Spirit. With the Scripture as the rule and the Spirit as the guide, Wesley worked out his theology. This chapter examines the history of the Wesleyan Quadrilateral and analyzes the role of the Holy Spirit in each of the four areas.

Scripture, tradition, reason and experience are ways in which God continues to tell His story to man. Through them, He speaks to us and lets us know we are not alone, but He is with us. The Holy Spirit is the initiator of this divine conversation between God and man. The Quadrilateral is a theological method John Wesley used to understand the work and Word of God. Since this took place through the role of the Holy Spirit, believers must have the Spirit's guidance to search for a more "Scriptural Christianity."

The term *Wesleyan Quadrilateral* does not appear in the writings of John Wesley. It is a term Albert C. Outler used to describe Wesley's theological method. In fact, Outler regretted having coined it, because it has been so widely misconstrued.[1] Nonetheless, it remains a helpful aid for understanding the context of Wesleyan thought. We can see in Wesley a distinctive theological method, with Scripture as its norm and tradition, reason, and Christian experience as aids for the interpretation of the Word of God.

John Wesley offered no creed or catechism for his people to follow. In fact, he did not articulate an explicit theological method because he was more concerned with practical relevance and applicable theology.[2] He has been called a practical theologian because he wanted every ordinary woman and man to be able to understand the Scriptures. He wrote, "I desire plain truth for plain people."

This does not mean Wesley was not a theologian because he did not write a systematic theology. On the contrary, Wesley's refusal to provide the Methodists with a confession was the conviction of a man who knew his own mind on every vexed question of Christian doctrine, but who had decided that the reduction of doctrine to any particular form of words was to misunderstand the very nature of doctrinal statements.[3] Some argue that Wesley was indeed a systematic theologian whose sermons, essays, journals, prefaces and letters contain every major point of a systematic theology.

Wesley's distinctiveness rests not in a systematic theology, but in a theological method.[4] His uniqueness of thought is evident in the way he was able to use his theological method to get his people to theologize for themselves. The effect of this was to make every Methodist man and woman his or her own theologian, not by giving them an actual paradigm for their theologizing, but hoping that they would adopt his way of reflection as their own.[5] Therefore, his genius was not in writing a catechism or systematic theology, but in allowing his people to "think and let think" in a way that was consistent with the written Word of God and doctrinal authority.

Having briefly introduced the purpose and nature of John Wesley's theological method, we will now examine each of the four areas of the Wesleyan Quadrilateral: Scripture, tradition, reason and experience. Each one is uniquely important and vital to the Christian faith because there is a need today for an approach to theology that has the capability to dynamically fuse the four historical sources of Wesley's theological method together in order to bring us into contemporary dialogue with other traditions. As we look at each area individually, the role of the Holy Spirit will be further examined.

SCRIPTURE

John Wesley appealed to Scripture for all doctrinal authority. He believed the "written word of God to be the only and sufficient rule both of Christian faith and practice."[6] Both Reformation and Anglican heritage taught *sola Scriptura*, which no doubt influenced

Wesley's love for the Bible. Once Wesley's view of the Bible is taken into proper perspective, one can begin to understand his theological method.

In the Quadrilateral, the Scriptures stand first, while tradition, reason and Christian experience are used as a means for understanding the Scriptures. The latter three provide lenses by which we can interpret and understand the written word of God more clearly. The Scriptures assist believers on their journey of faith as they press on toward perfection. There is a dynamic interplay in which tradition, reason and experience work to shine light on Scripture. They have a unique reciprocal interrelationship, while Scripture always remains first. Although never a substitute for Scripture, tradition, reason and experience are complementary to its interpretation.

Wesley was not a novice in his understanding of the original languages of the Bible. He translated both the Old and New Testaments from their original tongues into English. He felt that it was important for his preachers to have knowledge of all of the Scriptures. Wesley's love for the Holy Scriptures can be best described in his own words:

> Concerning the Scriptures in general, it may be observed, the word of the Living God, which directed the first patriarchs also, was, in the time of Moses, committed to writing. To this were added, in several succeeding generations, the inspired writings of the other prophets. Afterward, what the Son of God preached, and the Holy Ghost spake by the apostles, the apostles and wrote. This is what we now style the Holy Scripture: this is that Word of God which remaineth forever: of

which, though heaven and earth pass away, one jot or title shall not pass away. The Scripture therefore of the Old and New Testament is a most solid and precious system of Divine truth. Every part thereof is worthy of God; and all together are one entire body, wherein is no defect, no excess. It is the fountain of heavenly wisdom, which they who are able to taste, prefer to all writings of men, however wise, or learned, or holy.[8]

Spirit and Scripture

Wesley firmly believed that the Holy Spirit inspired Scripture. He took this a step further in saying, "The Spirit of God not only once inspired those who wrote it, but continually inspires—supernaturally assists—those who read it with earnest prayer."[9]

He believed that God continually speaks and inspires the reader of the Bible through the inner working of the Spirit. This is a dual inspiration, where the Holy Spirit *inspired* the ancient writers of the Scriptures and *inspires* the contemporary readers that they may comprehend the Word of God. We see the Spirit's hermeneutical work beautifully described in Hymn 255:

Spirit of truth, essential God,
Who didst thy ancient saints inspire,
Shed in their hearts thy love abroad,
And touch their hallowed lips with fire;
Our God from all eternity,
World without end we worship thee!

Still we believe, almighty Lord,
Whose presence fills both earth and heaven,
The meaning of the written word

Is by thy inspiration given;
Thou only dost thyself explain the secret mind
of God to man.

Come, then, divine Interpreter,
The scriptures to our hearts apply;
And, taught by thee, we God revere,
Him in Three Persons magnify;
In each the Triune God adore,
Who was, and is for evermore.[10]

We still need the ongoing presence of the Holy Spirit in our reading of Scripture and our doctrine. Without the assistance of the Holy Spirit, our reading of the Bible will be in vain.

TRADITION

No one can doubt that John Wesley was a man who had a tremendous appreciation and reverence for Christian tradition. He used church tradition in his complex, theological method because he felt it would direct him to the strongest evidence for Christian doctrine. When examining the Wesleyan synthesis, we find several major traditions at work. The traditions that had the greatest influence on Wesley were Anglicanism, Moravianism, and the Eastern Fathers.[11]

It was Wesley's Anglican heritage more than any other that pointed him to the study of the early Church Fathers. There were also many cultural and religious tributaries, which formed John Wesley's eclectic use of tradition.[12] However, we will only examine two of the main influences on John Wesley's theological development at this point—Anglicanism and the Eastern Fathers.

Anglicanism was perhaps the greatest influence in shaping Wesley's view of church tradition. He was immersed in the social and religious culture of the Church of England. He grew up the son of an Anglican priest. From a young age, he read Anglican homilies and devotional literature. Three major English works that influenced Wesley were Bishop Taylor's *Rules and Exercises of Holy Living and Dying*, à Kempis's *Christian's Pattern*, and Mr. Law's *Christian Perfection and Serious Call*. He was educated at Oxford and ordained to the Anglican priesthood. His love for the Church of England can also be seen in the fact that he never wanted Methodism to become a separate church, but to bring renewal to the Church of England.

Throughout the *Works of John Wesley* are numerous mentions of the early Church Fathers, the "primitive Church", and "Christian antiquity". "Christian antiquity", as he sometimes called it, served a major role in his theological approach to interpreting the Scriptures. He said, "I reverence their writings, because they describe true, genuine Christianity, and direct us to the strongest evidence of the Christian doctrine."[13]

First and foremost, Wesley's concern and appreciation of early-church tradition was a hermeneutical one. He believed that a renewal of early-church studies would help renew the Church of England from within by pointing the way to a "true" religion of the heart. Wesley's hope and vision for a pure church gave birth to what was to become the next major link of church tradition.

Wesley saw Methodism as being a part of a long line of church tradition, which reflected a genuine Christianity. Donald A.D. Thorsen points out that Wesley traced the Methodist genealogy back to the "old religion."[14] Wesley describes Methodism as "the old religion, the religion of the Bible, the religion of the primitive church, the religion of the Church of England." For Wesley, Methodism was a part of an unbroken chain of true religion, religion of the heart, which was "no other than love, the love of God and of all mankind."[15] It is the tradition of "Methodism" as John Wesley intended it, that all Wesleyan-holiness churches would be able to trace their theological heritage.

Spirit and Tradition

The Holy Spirit played a unique role in John Wesley's understanding of church tradition. The Holy Spirit first inspired the Scriptures, and then He inspired the interpreters of the Scriptures. He viewed the early Fathers as "the most authentic commentators on Scripture" because they were "nearest to the fountain, and eminently endued with that Spirit by whom all Scripture was written."[16] Their authenticity as interpreters of Scripture was because they had been endued with the Spirit. Wesley believed deeply that being filled with the Spirit was the mark of "Scriptural Christianity." Therefore, the presence of the Holy Spirit in the early church vindicated that their interpretation of Scripture was valid.

REASON

It is important to understand John Wesley within the historical context of the 18th century. It was a time known as the Age of Reason or the Enlightenment, where truth could only be known through the use of reason, logic and scientific method. He was deeply influenced by the ideas of the Enlightenment, but he was also committed to the possibility of God's special revelation. He sought to logically join religion and reason. The way Wesley used reason to think rationally about religion can be traced to his Anglican background. He studied both Aristotelian logic and the empirical philosophy of John Locke, applying their lessons to his ministry and theology.

Wesley spent a considerable amount of time trying to explain the relationship between reason and religion. He attempted to find a middle ground between extremists who valued one over the other. For Wesley, "reason is much the same with understanding. It means a faculty of the human soul; that faculty which exerts itself in three ways—by simple apprehension, by judgment, and by discourse."[17]

To the consideration of what reason cannot do, Wesley again offers three things: "First, reason cannot produce faith. Secondly, reason alone cannot produce hope in any child of man: I mean scriptural hope. Thirdly, reason, however cultivated and improved, cannot produce the love of God"[18] Wesley made a clear distinction between what reason could and could not do. Although he valued reason greatly, he realized that it was of secondary importance and useless speculation without God.

Spirit and Reason

Throughout the course of his life, John Wesley attempted to reconcile the role of reason and religion. Intuition or deductive reasoning alone cannot lead a person to the revelation of God; the Holy Spirit must be present and actively working in the believer. In "The Case of Reason Considered," John Wesley asks:

"Is it not reason (assisted by the Holy Ghost) which enables us to understand what the Holy Scriptures declare concerning the being and attributes of God?" and then he states, "It is by this we understand (His Spirit opening and enlightening the eyes of our understanding)."[19] Wesley explicitly states that the Holy Spirit must assist our reasoning if we are to understand the things of God.

Elsewhere, Wesley declared, "You cannot reason concerning spiritual things, if you have no spiritual sight; because all your ideas received by your outward senses are of a different kind." Wesley continues, "This cannot be till the Almighty come into your succour, and give you that faith you have hitherto despised. Then upborne, as it were, on eagles' wings, you shall soar away into the regions of eternity; and your enlightened reason shall explore even 'the deep things of God'; God himself 'revealing them to you by his Spirit.'"[20] For Wesley, spiritual sight is only possible when the Holy Spirit opens and enlightens our spiritual understanding.

EXPERIENCE

The restoration of religious experience to the Christian faith is perhaps John Wesley's most significant theological contribution. Scripture, tradition and reason were common theological methods used by Roman Catholics and Anglicans in Wesley's day. What this three-part method lacked was a spiritual confirmation, or an assurance of salvation within the heart, mind and soul of the believer. John Wesley saw the need for a reappropriation of Christian experience;

once it was recovered, it soon became one of the distinctive marks of Methodism. He said of experience that "a great evangelical truth has been recovered, which had been for many years well-nigh lost and forgotten."[21] Experience was a jewel Wesley placed back into the crown of Christianity.

Through a series of encounters with a group called the Moravians, John Wesley became aware that he lacked the experience of Christian assurance. This led him to an intense introspection of his personal faith in Christ, where he began to realize that he did not have the inner "witness of the Spirit." Through searching the Scriptures, self-analysis, and continued dialogue with other living witnesses of "an instantaneous work," Wesley was now ready to receive the experiential faith.

Christian experience is a personal, first hand encounter with the living God, who gives us the "witness of the Spirit." John Wesley described this in the following way: "The testimony of the Spirit is an inward impression on the soul, whereby the Spirit of God directly witnesses to my spirit, that I am a child of God."[22]

The inward "impression" on the soul does not refer to feelings per se, but a complex synergism that involves both feelings and intuition. Experience first involves God through His saving acts, and then the person who receives and perceives the reality of this action through all of the human faculties.

Spirit and Experience

John Wesley believed that the Holy Spirit was the primary agent involved in Christian experience. The Spirit awakens, assures, purifies and guides the believer in the way of salvation. In "A Letter to a Roman Catholic," he writes:

> I believe the infinite and eternal Spirit of God,
> equal with the Father and the Son, to be not only
> perfectly holy in himself but the immediate cause
> of all holiness in us; enlightening our understand-
> ings, rectifying our wills and affections, renewing
> our natures, uniting our persons to Christ, assur-
> ing us of the adoption of sons, leading us in our
> actions; purifying and sanctifying our souls and
> bodies, to a full and eternal enjoyment of God.[23]

"The Spirit itself beareth witness with our spirit, that we are the children of God" (Romans 8:16). Wesley used this scripture to give an explication of the work the Spirit does in His children. The Spirit who inspired the Scriptures continuously works to confirm the experiential truths found within its texts. In fact, Wesley believed that the witness of the Spirit confirmed what the Scriptures taught concerning experience. He said, "What the Scripture promises, I enjoy. Come and see what Christianity has done here; and acknowledge it is of God."[24]

Experience can be verified inwardly and outwardly. The immediate result of this testimony is the fruit of the Spirit. Wesley believed that without the fruit of the Spirit, the testimony of the Spirit couldn't continue. Both the witness and fruit of the Spirit spring forth from an experiential relationship with Jesus Christ. The Holy Spirit is the One who initiates a divine encounter where man can experience God. The Spirit also works to give the witness and fruit of the Spirit to believers so we may know that we are children of God.

Lessons for Today

The Holy Spirit works in numerous ways to bring humanity into the full knowledge of the saving faith in Jesus Christ, the Son of God. Colin W. Williams describes the Spirit's work in the following way:

> The Spirit speaks to us through the Scripture which he uses as his final authority; but to give us a vital awareness of the revelation there recorded, he calls to witness the believers through whom he has spoken to the Church in time past, and the believers in whom his promises are being realized now. And while the Spirit works in a variety of ways, the promises of God are changeless, and therefore there is a "common salvation" offered to all, which it is the task of theology and preaching to describe.[25]

This "common salvation" is at the heart of Wesley's theology and theological method. As this article demonstrated, there is a distinct role of the Holy Spirit in the Wesleyan Quadrilateral. One cannot separate the Quadrilateral from the work of the Holy Spirit.

The Holy Spirit uses the four religious sources: Scripture, tradition, reason and experience to guide the believer in the way of salvation. With the Scripture as the rule and the Spirit as the Guide, the same Spirit who initiated them must interpret reason, tradition and experience. Without the Spirit, each source is void of any discernable religious truth. Thus, there must be the inspiration and supernatural assistance of the Holy Spirit for believers to be able to understand the Scriptures and religious experiences.

The Holy Spirit runs throughout Wesley's writings, which can show that theological method can be "practical." He used the phrase "practical divinity" to refer to deep pastoral concerns that focused on nurturing the Christian life. He was more concerned with practical discipline than speculative academic theology. This can be seen in the titles and contents of his sermons, hymns and letters. At the heart of his practical theology is his doctrine of the Holy Spirit that offers us an approach to theological method that can and should be an encounter with the living God. We are not just studying about God, but we are seeking to know Him personally through a spiritual approach to theology that involves the Spirit.

We should be open to the freedom of the Spirit and respect His work in church tradition. Whether it is Catholic, Methodist, Episcopal or Pentecostal, each tradition should not be separated from the work of the Spirit. With this in mind, Christians should practice fellowship across the traditions, because the Holy Spirit has been with all God's people in all traditions in all centuries.[26] Thus, a spiritual approach to tradition can and should inform our theology past, present and future.

The contribution of Wesley's theological method for Christians is not that it is exclusively Wesleyan, but that it is explicitly ecumenical. It does not point to Wesley himself, but it brings us into dialogue with various other traditions—both ancient and contemporary. Wesley points us away from himself to the church at large, the church of all ages, both then and now. The Wesleyan Quadrilateral forces us to hold in tension various views from different Christian traditions.

Wesley can help us better understand our own heritage and place within the body of Christ. No one Christian group has a perfect system of doing theology.

We can and should learn from one another. Yes, Arminians can even learn from the Calvinists. The evangelical community needs both George Whitefield and John Wesley to achieve the beauty of balance.[27] With this in mind, Wesley becomes a good dialogue partner for embarking on a pilgrimage in theological method because he was not afraid to look to the Holy Spirit and the larger Christian family for help along the journey.

> I will conclude all with that excellent Collect of our Church: "O God, who in all ages has taught the hearts of thy faithful people, by sending them the light of thy Holy Spirit; grant us by the same Spirit to have a right judgment in all things, and ever more to rejoice in his holy comfort, through the merits of Jesus Christ our Saviour; who liveth and reigneth with thee, in the unity of the same Spirit, one God, world without end. Amen."[28]

REFLECTION QUESTIONS

1. How can you utilize the Wesleyan Quadrilateral in your life and theology? Do you already use it now?

2. What elements of the Quadrilateral do you think are more important than others? Explain why and how.

3. Is it important to have a theological method? Do most people recognize this need? Explain why and how.

4. Is there anything you would take from or add to the Wesleyan Quadrilateral? Please explain your answer.

Endnotes

[1] Albert C. Outler, "The Wesleyan Quadrilateral in John Wesley," *Wesleyan Theological Journal* 20:1 (Spring 1985).

[2] Donald A.D. Thorsen, *The Wesleyan Quadrilateral: Scripture, Tradition, Reason, and Experience as a Model of Evangelical Theology* (Grand Rapids: Zondervan, 1990) 16.

[3] Outler, *Wesleyan Quadrilateral*, 2.

[4] Thorsen, 7.

[5] Outler, *Wesleyan Quadrilateral*, 4.

[6] *Works*, 8:340.

[7] *Works*, 5:3.

[8] John Wesley, Preface. *Explanatory Notes Upon the New Testament (Salem, Ohio: Schumal, 2000) 5.*

[9] John Wesley, *Explanatory Notes Upon the New Testament*, 2 Timothy 3:16.

[10] John and Charles Wesley, *A Collection of Hymns for the Use of the People Called Methodists*, ed. Franz Hildebrant and Oliver A. Beckerlegge, vol. 7 in the *Bicentennial Edition of the Works of John Wesley* (Nashville: Abingdon, 1989) Hymn 255.

[11] Kenneth J. Collins, "John Wesley's Critical Appropriation of Tradition in His Practical Theology," *Wesleyan Theological Journal* 35:2 (2000): 69-90.

[12] Ted A. Campbell, *John Wesley and Christian Antiquity: Religious Vision and Cultural Change* (Nashville: Kingswood, 1991).

[13] *Works*, 10:79.

[14] Thorsen, 152.

[15] *Works*, 7:423.

[16] *Works*, 10:485.

[17] *Works*, 6:353.

[18] *Works*, 6:355-58.

[19] *Works*, 6:354.

[20] *Works*, 8:14.

[21] *Works*, 5:124.

[22] *Works*, 5:124.

[23] *Works*, 10:82.

[24] *Works*, 10:79.

[25] Colin W. Williams, *John Wesley's Theology Today* (Nashville: Abingdon, 1960) 37.

[26] Jim Packer, taken from lecture given at Wheaton College on "The Bible in America," cited in Roger Steer, *Guarding the Holy Fire: The Evangelicalism of John R.W. Stott, J.I. Packer, and Alister McGrath* (Grand Rapids: Baker, 1999) 218.

[27] Olson, Roger E., "Don't Hate Me Because I'm Arminian," *Christianity Today*, Sept. 6, 1999.

[28] *Works*, 7:520.

part three

John Wesley's
Legacy

* * * * * * *

AND ARE WE YET ALIVE

And are we yet alive,
And see each other's face?
Glory and praise to Jesus give
For his redeeming grace!
Preserved by power divine
To full salvation here,
Again in Jesu's praise we join,
And in his sight appear.

What troubles have we seen,
What conflicts have we past,
Fightings without, and fears within,
Since we assembled last!
But out of all the Lord
Hath brought us by his love;
And still he doth his help afford,
And hides our life above.

Then let us make our boast
Of his redeeming power,
Which saves us to the uttermost,
Till we can sin no more:
Let us take up the cross,
Till we the crown obtain;
And gladly reckon all things loss,
So we may Jesus gain.

chapter ten

Wesleyan Movement

J ohn Wesley's lasting legacy is demonstrated by the amazing spread of Methodism throughout the world. Methodism grew from just a handful of students at Oxford College in 1726 to nearly 45,000 followers at the time of Wesley's death in 1791. In only a few short years, the numbers increased to over 200,000 members strong. Methodism then gave birth to numerous other denominations, which today have nearly 40,000,000 members worldwide. Wesley's followers have faithfully and successfully fulfilled his challenge to spread Scriptural holiness throughout the world. This chapter looks at the general spread of the Methodist revival, examines several of the main contemporary Wesleyan movements, and then conclude with an application of Wesley's influence on these movements today.

BRITISH METHODISM

After Wesley's death, the British Methodists took steps to become fully autonomous from the Church of

England. In 1795, they drew up the "plan of pacifica-
tion," which gave them the right to perform many of
the ordinary functions of a legitimate church. This
allowed them to practice the sacraments and bury the
dead with the approval of the majority of the preachers
of the Conference.

By 1836, Methodist preachers received full ordination, making the separation from the Church of England
complete. In 1848, membership in Great Britain had
grown to 338,861 and 23,842 in Ireland. As the years pro-
gressed, so did the development and growth of British
Methodism. Their numbers have continued to grow
and out of their ranks have come various church bodies,
including the Salvation Army, which was founded by
William Booth in the later 19th century. Also, an independent Methodist Conference exists in Ireland, which
was established by Wesley himself.

Missions

As a result of British Methodism's missionary out-
reaches, there are conferences throughout the world. In
the Pacific, there are independent conferences in
Australia, New Zealand and Tonga. Methodism in the
West Indies is associated with Thomas Coke, who
desired to take Methodism to the East, but died at sea
in 1814 on his way to Ceylon. His ministry companions
established the work in Ceylon that spread into India.

In 1811, Sierra Leone became the site of the first
Methodist work in West Africa. In South Africa,
Methodism has an independent conference that was
created in 1882. Missions also came to Burma and China
in the late 1800s. Today, British Methodism has almost
1,200,000 members throughout the various churches.

AMERICAN METHODISM

As in England, John Wesley was the one who laid the foundation for American Methodism. Its official organization occurred at the historic "Christmas Conference" on December 24, 1784, in Baltimore, Maryland. The Conference named Francis Asbury and Thomas Coke cosuperintendents, and adopted the name Methodist Episcopal Church. From that time forth, Francis Asbury, not Wesley, is seen as the father of the American church. Once Asbury took leadership, he pushed the American church forward to expand its boundaries into territories that had not been reached by any Christian group. As a result of his leadership, Methodism organized Methodist circuits, ordained preachers, increased the number of the Annual Conference, divided the conference into districts, held revivals and camp meetings in various parts of the country, founded schools and colleges, gathered members from all races and classes, and established churches throughout the nation.

Divisions and Unity

Over time, there were several major splits within American Methodists, which resulted in the formation of various Methodist church bodies. A serious split occurred in 1830. In order to restrict the power of the bishops and create a stronger democracy, the Methodist Protestant Church was formed. Then in the 1840s, another split occurred over the issue of slavery. The roots of this division went back to 1784, when the Conference outlawed slavery in the Methodist Episcopal Church.

In 1844, Bishop James Andrew had taken a wife who owned slaves. Rather than resigning, he became the leader of the Southern Methodists who were in favor of slavery. A plan of separation was made and in Louisville, Kentucky, in May 1845, the Methodist Episcopal Church South was organized. The Southern church began with a membership of 460,000.

Around 1870, there was a move toward healing between the North and South of the major Methodist divisions. Although it took a number of years to work out issues over government and property, the two churches gradually became unified. A commission made up of representatives of the Methodist Episcopal Church, Methodist Episcopal Church South, and the Methodist Protestant Church formed a plan of union, which became a reality in 1939. The united conference was composed of 900 delegates from each denomination. They met in Kansas City, Missouri, and unanimously adopted the Declaration of Union, becoming the Methodist Church. This body merged in 1968 with the Evangelical United Brethren to become what is now known as the United Methodist Church.

The United Methodist Church is the largest Methodist body in America, with over 11,000,000 members and 36,771 local churches within the United States and 1,157,816 members outside of the U.S. There are 68 annual conferences in the U.S. and 48 annual conferences outside of the U.S. There are five jurisdictional conferences established for geographical convenience. Their general conference consists of 1,000 delegates, made up of half laity and half clergy. Bishops are elected for life and constitute the Council of Bishops that meet at least once a year. There are 87 United Methodist colleges and universities and 13 seminaries. The church is also active in 79 countries, with missions in Latin America, India, China, Africa, Pakistan, Japan, Korea, the Philippines, Asia and Europe.

Black Methodists

Before the emancipation, there were no official black churches in the South, but in the North two independent black churches had been formed before the Civil War. The African Methodist Episcopal Church began in 1787, in Philadelphia. Richard Allen, a black minister, wanted blacks to have their own place of worship. He purchased an old frame building that had been a blacksmith's shop and used it for a house of worship. It was formally organized in 1816, under Allen's leadership. Allen was also ordained and consecrated as the church's first bishop by Francis Asbury. The AME Church quickly grew to 7,500 members in the 1820s. It has become one of the largest Methodist churches in the United States, with nearly 3,300,000 members in 7,200 churches today.

The African Methodist Episcopal Zion Church dates from 1796. This was organized by a group who protested racial discrimination in New York. The first church, Zion, was built in 1800. The AME Zion Church held its first annual conference in 1821 and James Varick was elected the first bishop. The AME Zion Church spread quickly throughout the Northern states and grew rapidly in the 1860s. Today, their membership is nearly 1,200,000 in 3,000 churches worldwide.

Wesleyan-Holiness Churches

During the 1800s there were several churches that broke off from Methodism over the issue of holiness and began to form their own denominations. Churches such as the Church of God (Anderson, Indiana), Church of the Nazarene, Church of God (Holiness), the Salvation Army, the Wesleyan Methodist Church, and

the Free Methodist Church all grew out of the
Wesleyan-Holiness Movement of the 19th century.
These Holiness churches are joined together by membership in the Christian Holiness Association which
was founded after the Civil War by a group of ministers
to promote Christian holiness.

The Salvation Army is the largest Holiness church
with nearly 1,500,000 members. Its founder, William
Booth, was an ordained Methodist minister in England
who left the church to dedicate his life and ministry to
the poverty-stricken masses of London. He began the
work under the name Christian Mission, but in 1878, the
name was changed to the Salvation Army. The new
organization was set up on a military pattern where
members were soldiers, ministers were officers, converts
were seekers, and Booth was the general. The Salvation
Army was a great revival movement in the late 1800s. It
quickly spread through the British Isles and into the
United States in 1880. Today they are mostly known for
their benevolent ministry. They have boys' and girls'
clubs, medical facilities, programs for homeless, and
rehabilitation centers—all given to help people in need.

The Church of the Nazarene is the second largest of
these Holiness churches with nearly 1,400,000 members in 10,882 churches worldwide. The church was
the result of the merger of three independent Holiness
groups forming the Pentecostal Church of the
Nazarene. Then in 1919, Pentecostal was dropped
from the name, leaving it the Church of the Nazarene.
The church's doctrine and polity is Wesleyan with a
strong emphasis on justification and entire sanctification of believers. The Church of the Nazarene is also
dedicated to world missions and evangelism. The

church has eight liberal arts colleges and universities in the U.S. and 26 colleges and seminaries throughout the world.

World Methodist Council

Many of the Wesleyan churches we have just discussed are members of the World Methodist Council, which was formed in 1881 to bring closer fellowship to the various churches in the worldwide Wesleyan Movement. Its headquarters are located at Lake Junaluska, North Carolina. The World Council has held 15 ecumenical conferences and has become increasingly active in uniting the Wesleyan Movement in recent years. Its mission is to . . .

- Deepen fellowship
- Foster Methodist participation in the ecumenical movement
- Advance unity of theological and moral standards
- Suggest priorities in Methodist activity
- Promote effective use of Methodist resources in the Christian mission
- Encourage evangelism
- Promote Christian education
- Pray for and support needs of persecuted Christians
- Encourage ministries of justice and peace
- Study union and reunion proposals which affect member churches
- Sponsor a minister exchange program
- Encourage the development of worship and liturgical life in member churches
- Coordinate and support worldwide Methodist publishing interests.

The World Methodist Council represents 54,000,000 adherents worldwide.

Lessons for Today

Although there is a lot of diversity in the various Wesleyan movements, they all share one thing in common—their ancestor, John Wesley. Different Wesleyan groups have emphasized different things that have originated from Wesley's polity, ministry and theology. Some churches are Wesleyan in polity, while others are Wesleyan in doctrine.

The various Wesleyan movements represent a unique heritage of unity and diversity that can be seen in the universal body of Christ. Although there are differences, there are a lot of similarities. It is like going to a family reunion and seeing your cousins for the first time. Although you have never met them before, you can see a distinguishable family resemblance. Wesleyan churches are like cousins who should take the time to get to know one another.

REFLECTION QUESTIONS

1. What is your first impression having read a little bit about the various Wesleyan movements?

2. What is the most interesting thing you have learned about the Methodist church, both past and present?

3. What do you think the original Methodist men and women would think about the Methodism today?

4. Are there any ways you think the Wesleyan heritage should be renewed in the church today? Explain your answer.

5. How do you think Wesleyanism has spread from just a handful of people in England to a worldwide movement?

6. What are some of the important things all of the Wesleyan churches have in common?

chapter eleven

Wesley and the Pentecostals

Pentecostalism is what some might call the forgotten legacy of John Wesley. In nearly 100 years, the movement has become the fastest-growing body of Christians on the face of the planet. Pentecostalism is growing at a rate of 13 million a year, 35,000 a day, with almost a half billion followers. It is the second largest Christian group after Roman Catholicism.

There are Pentecostals in almost every denomination and every part of the world. The largest Protestant church in the world is a Pentecostal church in Korea, the Yoido Full Gospel Church, which has over 240,000 in weekly attendance. All of this would not have been possible without their theological and ministerial connection to John Wesley. This chapter briefly discusses the historical development of Pentecostalism by making a special application of John Wesley's contribution.

A lot of research has shown the connection between the Wesleyan-Holiness Movement and Pentecostalism.[1] Much of this research has attempted to show that John Wesley is the grandfather of Pentecostalism.[2] Wesley placed a strong emphasis on the person and work of the Holy Spirit. He believed the Spirit played a unique role in entire sanctification. Wesley's doctrine of Christian perfection was crucial to the theological roots of Pentecostalism. It was the idea of a second work of grace (sanctification) that opened the door for theological discussion about the possibilities of a third work of grace: the baptism with the Holy Spirit.

Wesleyan Sanctification

Shortly after his memorial sermon, "On the Death of George Whitefield," preached on November 18, 1770, Wesley entered into a unique alliance with John Fletcher that shifted the direction of Methodist history.[3] Fletcher worked closely with Wesley and soon became one of the most influential leaders in early Methodism. Fletcher is perhaps best noted for his *Checks to Antinomianism* (1771), which defended the theological views of John Wesley and the early Methodism. Wesley was so impressed by Fletcher's piety and theological prowess that Fletcher became his "authorized interpreter and designated successor."[4]

In Fletcher's writings, we begin to see a paradigm shift take place. Fletcher placed a strong emphasis on the role of the Holy Spirit in Christian perfection. He used Pentecostal language to describe the Spirit's work, with phrases such as "baptized with the Spirit" and "filled with the Spirit."

As a result of Fletcher's influence, Wesley's latter sermons "highlighted the Methodist phenomenon as inaugurating a 'Pentecostal Church' in the world."[5] The distinct contribution Fletcher made on Wesley's theology was the concept of a "Pentecostal Church," which helped Wesley articulate and defend the extraordinary work of God that was happening through the Methodist Movement.

Larry Wood notes that Wesley's latter sermons focused on a Pentecostal theme because he believed the Methodist revival in his day was the first sign of a new Pentecost. He believed that a new Pentecostal Church was being reestablished on the earth that would be the fulfillment of the first Pentecost.[6]

The external evidence of the outward work of the Spirit resembled the first Pentecost and demonstrated that God was indeed with the Methodists as they spread universally throughout the world. Wesley's concept of a Pentecostal Church demonstrated a growing interest in the universal work of the Spirit and marked a further shift in Wesley's doctrine of the Holy Spirit.

Holiness Movement

Both Wesley and Fletcher's writings were widely spread among early Methodists and became distributed widely in the later Holiness Movement. The Holiness Movement of the 1800s served as the major catalyst for the spread of the doctrine of entire sanctification. The Movement emphasized sanctification as a second definite work of grace, which is distinct from salvation. Various terms were used to describe this experience beyond conversion, including *Christian perfection, entire sanctification, second blessing,* and *higher Christian life.*

The Holiness Movement helped spread the message of the second blessing throughout North America and Europe through camp meetings and conventions like the National Holiness Association. These camp meetings were literally held in major cities and states across the country. Many of the Holiness people were prolific writers and theologians who promoted the spread of the doctrine of entire sanctification in their writings and teachings. Although the Holiness Movement was made up of various denominations, Methodism played an important role in the beginning of the Movement. In the late 1800s the Movement began to split into various independent Holiness churches. Despite divisions, all of them agreed on the prominent role of the Holy Spirit in entire sanctification.

The Holiness Movement helped contribute to the shift from an emphasis on entire sanctification to a growing emphasis on Spirit baptism. The change did not take place overnight, but it was the result of various Christian groups who sought to find new ways of appropriating and articulating the role of the Holy Spirit in Christian experience. There are several key leaders who contributed to the emphasis on Spirit baptism and sanctification.

Revivalist Charles Finney was a powerful preacher and teacher in the mid-1800s. He was practicing law when he experienced a dramatic conversion, after which he gave up everything to pursue the call to preach. Finney soon emerged as the new leader of evangelical revivalism. His revivals burned through major urban areas like Philadelphia, New York City, Boston and Rochester. His fame brought him international attention that eventually took him to England.

He was influenced by the Wesleyan theology of Christian perfectionism, which developed from the teaching of John Wesley. "One of Finney's theological innovations was his increasing tendency to identify the baptism of the Holy Spirit as a means of entering

into entire sanctification."[7] He identified entire sanctification with the baptism of the Holy Spirit, which
connects him to both Wesleyan-Holiness and later,
Pentecostal thought.[8]

Finney's work on perfectionism was sparked by the
problem of converts who became backsliders after his
revivals. Holiness made it possible for the believer to
live a life for God that was free from sin. He thought
that believers needed the baptism with the Holy Spirit
to empower and perfect them that they might live in
accordance to the will of God. He emphasized the
need for purity and power. He argued that it was the
duty of Christians to be filled with the Spirit:

> (1) It is your duty because you have a promise of
> it. (2) Because God has commanded it. (3) It is
> essential to your own growth in grace that you
> should be filled with the Spirit. (4) It is as impor-
> tant that you should be sanctified. (5) It is as nec-
> essary as it is that you should be useful and do
> good in the world. (6) If you do not have the
> Spirit of God in you, you will dishonor God, dis-
> grace the church, and be lost. [9]

Finney drew on Wesley's doctrine of Christian perfectionism by adding an emphasis on the baptism with
the Spirit, which helped make the shift for the later
development of the Pentecostal Movement.

Another influential Holiness teacher was Phoebe
Palmer, who taught that sanctification was attainable in
an instant. She was a Methodist lay preacher, revivalist
and Christian feminist. She developed an "altar theology," where she reduced the process of sanctification
into an instantaneous event. She reasoned that if her
body were a living sacrifice, by laying her all on the

altar, then God would sanctify her. She developed a three-step process for entire sanctification:

1. Consecrating oneself to God
2. Believing God keeps His promise to sanctify the consecrated
3. Bearing witness to what God has done

To promote her views of sanctification, she wrote the following books: *The Altar Covenant* (1837), *The Way of Holiness* (1843), and *Entire Devotion to God* (1845).

She also popularized the idea of Pentecostal Spirit baptism. Based on the Book of Acts' "Promise of the Father," she taught that Christians should wait for the promised Holy Spirit of Pentecost—available to both men and women. Although she never spoke in tongues, her emphasis on Pentecostal Spirit baptism helped prepare the way for the later emergence of the Pentecostal Movement.

As a result of Finney and Palmer's teaching, an emphasis on Spirit baptism began to take precedence over earlier views of sanctification. The Holiness teaching set the stage for the Pentecostal revival that started in 1906.

Azusa Street and Beyond

It was at the Azusa Street Mission in Los Angeles, California, where Pentecostalism found its fullest expression. Black minister William Seymour came under the influence of Holiness teaching around 1900 while he was living in Cincinnati. In 1903 he moved to Houston, Texas, where he came into contact with Charles Fox Parham. Parham was a Holiness teacher who began to teach that the Bible evidence of the baptism in the Holy Spirit was speaking in tongues. Parham established a Bible school to train students in the "Apostolic Faith." Because he was black, Seymour listened to lectures through the door by sitting in the hallway.

Parham worked tirelessly to promote the Pentecostal message. He started Bible schools to train ministers and orphanages. He began writing *The Apostolic Faith*. While studying the Acts of the Apostles, Parham and his students became convinced that God wanted to pour out a second Pentecost on them that would follow speaking in tongues.

One night with about 120 people gathered in the upper room of Parham's Bible School. Agnes Ozman asked Parham to lay hands on her to receive the gift of the Spirit. When Parham reluctantly agreed, she began to speak in tongues, making her the first person in the Pentecostal Movement to speak in tongues.[10] This became the spark that ignited the flames of the Pentecostal message.

Although he had not personally experienced it, Seymour accepted Parham's teaching of being baptized with the Spirit with the evidence of speaking in tongues. In 1906, Seymour was invited to help Julia Hutchins, a black Holiness pastor in Los Angeles. She did not receive Seymour's Pentecostal message and would not allow him to assist her or teach in the church. Seymour was then invited to the home of Richard Asberry at 214 Bonnie Brae Street. After months of prayer and fasting, Seymour and several others experienced the baptism with the Spirit with the evidence of tongues. The prayer meeting soon outgrew the little home, and they moved to an old abandoned African Methodist Episcopal Church on Azusa Street. They cleaned up the building and began to have services there. An amazing revival ensued.

Many people were influenced by the Pentecostal message of receiving the baptism of the Holy Ghost. As the influence of Azusa began to sweep through the United States, men and women came from all over the country to hear the full-gospel message (salvation, sanctification and Spirit baptism). Literally thousands experienced sanctification and Spirit baptism with the evidence of speaking in tongues. From Azusa Street, the Pentecostal message spread literally around the world.

Many denominations were directly impacted and influenced. Frank Bartleman traveled the East coast, spreading the message of Pentecost. G.B. Cashwell preached the Pentecostal message throughout the Southeast, influencing numerous denominations including the Church of God (Cleveland, Tennessee), the Freewill Baptist Church and the Fire Baptized Church. Pentecostalism's influence was not limited to the United States; believers took the message throughout the world by evangelism and missions. The doctrine of sanctification and Spirit baptism was an essential part of the ministry, mission and message of the early Pentecostal church.

Holiness-Pentecostal Churches

There are several major Pentecostal denominations that are both Wesleyan-Holiness and Pentecostal. These churches maintain an emphasis on three works of grace (salvation, sanctification, Spirit baptism). The largest is the Church of God in Christ (COGIC), founded in 1897 by two ministers, C.H. Mason and C.P. Jones in Memphis, Tennessee. Mason was the true leader who quickly took the reigns of the new group. He was filled with the Holy Ghost at Azusa Street and returned to Memphis to spread the message of Pentecost throughout the South.

In the beginning the COGIC was an interracial denomination, but in 1913, many of the white ministers broke off to form the Assemblies of God. Mason continued to work on both sides of the racial lines, but the group eventually became mostly Afro-American. The COGIC is the largest black Pentecostal denomination in the world with nearly 8,000,000 members. The church has two schools, Saint Junior College and C.H. Mason Theological Seminary in Atlanta.

The next largest of the Holiness-Pentecostal churches is the Church of God (Cleveland, Tennessee), which has nearly 6,000,000 members throughout the world. It was first known as the Christian Union, and was led by Richard G. Spurling. In 1896 a Holiness revival broke out at the Shearer Schoolhouse near Camp Creek, North Carolina. During the revival, believers experienced sanctification and Spirit baptism with the evidence of speaking with other tongues. In 1903, a Quaker Bible salesman named A.J. Tomlinson became the leader of the new movement and the name was changed to Church of God. Under his leadership, the church grew and moved to Cleveland, Tennessee. Tomlinson began preaching Pentecostal doctrine as early as 1907, but he was not filled with the Holy Spirit until 1908 in a revival meeting, led by G.B. Cashwell.

In 1923, during a turbulent time in the history of the Church of God, A.J. Tomlinson was dismissed as overseer because of irregularities in his management of church affairs. He then left with some 2,000 members and founded the Church of God of Prophecy. The Church of God of Prophecy is also based in Cleveland, Tennessee, and has churches throughout the world.

Despite the early split, the two denominations maintain a close relationship of prayer, evangelism and collaboration. F.J. Lee took his place as general overseer and under his leadership the Church of God continued to grow. Today the Church of God is the larger of the two and has a worldwide constituency with missionaries in many parts of the world. It maintains Lee University and several colleges and the Church of God Theological Seminary.

The Pentecostal Holiness Church is one of the oldest Pentecostal denominations in the world. Organized in 1898 in Anderson, South Carolina, under the name Fire-Baptized Holiness Church, it was the result of a number of Holiness associations. This group was strongly influenced by Methodist polity and Holiness doctrine of entire sanctification. The Pentecostal Holiness Church retains the office of bishop and is divided into conferences. It has two colleges: Emanuel College in Franklin Springs, Georgia, and Southwestern College in Oklahoma City. It also has Holmes Theological Seminary in Greenville, South Carolina, which is one of the oldest Pentecostal schools in the world. The Pentecostal Holiness Church is in over 40 states and 90 countries, and has nearly 350,000 members worldwide.

Lessons for Today

Many Pentecostals do not even know about their connection to John Wesley. In fact, the doctrine of sanctification is seldom heard in Pentecostal churches anymore. An emphasis on Spirit baptism and spiritual gifts has taken precedence over the Holiness message, which played such an important role in the development of Pentecostalism.

Pentecostals should revisit their Holiness roots if they are going to continue to be a dynamic movement. Steven Land says, "Had there been no 18th-century Wesleyan and 19th-century Holiness movements, there would have been no 20th-century Pentecostalism; and Pentecostalism is at any rate inexplicable without this theological heritage."[11] The message of sanctification anticipates charismatic dimensions of the Christian faith because purity always precedes power.

John Wesley played an important role in the development of the Holiness-Pentecostal movements. His emphasis on the person and work of the Holy Spirit in sanctification paved the way for later theologians to develop the doctrine of a Pentecostal Spirit baptism. His doctrine of sanctification has a distinct contribution to make in the contemporary ecumenical movement.

The significance of rediscovering Wesley's emphasis on the Holy Spirit and sanctification can bridge gaps between Wesleyan movements and Pentecostals and create a forum for dialogue between Protestants and Roman Catholics. There is no telling what will happen when the church rediscovers Wesley's doctrine of Holiness.

REFLECTION QUESTIONS

1. How did John Wesley play an important role in the development of Pentecostalism?

2. What other Christian leaders helped create the emphasis on Spirit baptism?

3. Did you know about the Wesleyan-Holiness connection to Pentecostals? If not, what do you personally think about it?

4. In what ways do you think John Wesley can continue to play an important role in the Pentecostal Movement?

5. Should Pentecostals revisit their Holiness roots? Explain why or why not.

Endnotes

[1] There are a number of books and articles that have discussed the theological connection between the Holiness Movement and Pentecostalism, among which are the following: Donald Dayton, *Theological Roots of Pentecostalism* (New Jersey: Hendrickson, 1987); D. William Faupel, *The Everlasting Gospel: The Significance of Eschatology in the Development of Pentecostal Thought* (Sheffield, England: Sheffield Academic, 1996); Steven J. Land, *Pentecostal Spirituality: A Passion for the Kingdom* (Sheffield, England: Sheffield Academic, 1997); and Vinson Synan, *The Holiness-Pentecostal Tradition: Charismatic Movements in the Twentieth Century* (Grand Rapids: Eerdmans, 1997).

[2] Steven J. Land, *Pentecostal Spirituality*, 35.

[3] Larry Wood, *The Meaning of Pentecost in Early Methodism: Rediscovering John Fletcher as Wesley's Vindicator and Designated Successor* (Scarecrow, 2003) 9.

[4] Wood, see chapter 5, "Wesley's Authorized Interpreter and Designated Successor," 75-94.

[5] Wood, 10.

[6] Wood, 68.

[7] Vinson Synan, *The Holiness Pentecostal Tradition: Charismatic Movements in the Twentieth Century* (Grand Rapids: Eerdmans, 1997) 15.

[8] Henry H. Knight III "From Aldersgate to Azusa: Wesley and the Renewal of Pentecostal Spirituality," *Journal of Pentecostal Theology*, vol. 8 (April 1996): 82-98. The author says that the Holiness message and an emphasis on the Holy Spirit are major points of continuity between Phoebe Palmer and Charles Finney and both Wesley and Pentecostals.

[9] Charles Finney, *Lectures on Revivals of Religion* (Virginia Beach: CBN University Press, 1978) 108.

[10] S.E. Parham, *The Life of Charles F. Parham: Founder of the Apostolic Faith Movement* (Joplin, MO: Hunter, 1930) 52.

[11] Land, 49.

chapter twelve

John Wesley for Today

It is only fitting that a book of this nature would conclude with a chapter on the relevance of John Wesley for today. The preceding chapters have highlighted the importance of his life, ministry and message, but this chapter will make a special contemporary application of John Wesley for Christians everywhere.

One of Wesley's primary concerns was addressing the significant issues of the day in which he lived. Most of his life and ministry was spent working to make the world a better place for humanity. He was concerned with human rights issues and sought to abolish slavery, poverty and the mistreatment of women. Even his theology has important implications for personal and social transformation of society. He believed Christians had a responsibility to the world in which they lived. For him to do nothing about human suffering was not to be a Christian at all.

Many of the same issues of Wesley's day are still important today. He would want the contemporary church to confront the current issues facing the church now. He sought to bring renewal to the church of his day, which in turn could provide a model for church renewal in all ages.

Several specific things Wesley can offer the church today include: the implications of John Wesley's life and ministry by making a special application of stewardship, evangelism, lay ministry, holiness and the marks of a Methodist. These are universal principles for genuine Christianity everywhere.

Stewardship

Wesley felt that Christians should be good stewards with their money. To be a steward means that you have been entrusted with something that belongs to someone else. At the heart, Wesley's understanding of stewardship is that we are made stewards of God's money. As Christians we have a responsibility to God with our finances and possessions—especially Christians who live in North America or Eastern Europe. He wrote numerous sermons on the issue of money and stewardship, including "The Use of Money," "The Danger of Riches," "On Riches," and "The Danger of Increasing Riches." In the sermon on the "Use of Money," Wesley emphasized three things we should do in terms of stewardship of our finances: "Gain all you can, save all you can, so you can give all you can."[1] This was Wesley's concept of stewardship in a nutshell.

We should *gain all we can*. He taught his followers to work hard and gain all they could in the worldly goods. This could be called the Protestant work ethic. Through our hard work, we are to gain as much as we can and not spend our money unwisely. It is a blessing of God to be able to make money. However, our hard labor should never be at the expense of someone else. There is nothing wrong with gaining money if it is not misused. Christians should, in fact, work hard and make a lot of money. The American dream was built on the concept of making as much as you can, but Wesley said that this was not enough.

He went on to exhort that we should *save all we can*. We are not to waste anything that we gain, but we are to save it wisely. Many times people spend their finances on things that aren't even important to them. Consumerism is one of the greatest enemies of Christians everywhere. Wesley warns that too often we are tempted to spend our money on worldly things that gratify our flesh. We should be careful how we spend our money, especially since all of our money belongs to God anyway. We may save our money by asking the simple question, "Is this a want or is this a need?" By simply taking time to ask ourselves this question, we may become better stewards of God's money.

Having gained all you can, and saved all you can, then *give all you can*. This is perhaps the most radical concept of Wesley's stewardship. After you have provided basic essentials for yourself and your family (such as food, clothing and shelter), you should use your money to help those who are in need. There are many people who are in need in our own neighborhoods. There may be people who are needy in our families and even in our churches.

More than one way is available to give to those in need:

- Give to one of the many local or national charities that offer legitimate help to the needy.
- Offer your time and assistance by volunteering at a local homeless shelter or food pantry.
- Help start a food pantry at your church.

With so many needy people, this can seem overwhelming. The most efficient way to help is to choose one or more charities that are the most important to you and help in any way you can. The most important thing you can do is take action.

Evangelism

Robert Coleman chose a quote from John Wesley for the title of one of his books, "Nothing to Do but Save Souls." Saving souls was the heart of Wesley's ministry. He won thousands to the Lord and expected his followers to do the same. On the importance of winning souls, Wesley charged his preachers:

> You have nothing to do but to win souls. Therefore spend and be spent in this work. And go always, not only to those that want you, but to those that want you most. Observe: It is not your business to preach as many times, and to take care of this or that society; but to save as many souls as you can; to bring as many sinners as you possibly can to repentance, and with all your power to build them up in that holiness without which they cannot see the Lord.[2]

This is a call to all Christians, whether they are ministers or laypeople. Winning souls is more than a vocation—it is a lifestyle that should be a part of our everyday life. We can be soulwinners at work, at home, in the supermarket, at the gym or wherever we spend our time. When was the last time you won somebody to Jesus?

There are numerous ways we can become better soulwinners.

1. *Read the Bible.* The more you get the Word of God in you, the easier it will be to share your faith with others. One of the main reasons Wesley loved the Bible was because he knew it gave him wisdom for winning souls.

2. *Pray that God will give you the right opportunity and words to say to others.* You would be surprised how many opportunities there are to share your faith with others.

3. *Just do it.* I am a firm believer that nothing will ever get done until we act. Many times people never share their faith because of fear, but the Bible says, "God has not given us a spirit of fear; but of power, and of love, and of a sound mind" (see 2 Timothy 1:7). Move past all your fears and share your faith. It's like fishing—you don't know what the fish are biting until you cast your line into the water.

4. *The best way to win your friends and family to Jesus is by personal or friendship evangelism.* It is said that people don't care how much you know until they know how much you care. Being an authentic Christian day after day is the best way to win somebody to Jesus Christ. But the fact remains—we still have to throw the bait out there. To be a living witness does not remove our responsibility to verbally share our faith. We must give the message of salvation. The Bible says, "Faith cometh by hearing, and hearing by the word of God" (Romans 10:17). Nothing can replace the power of the Word of God.

Lay Ministry

Most people don't realize that John Wesley did more for lay ministry than any other Christian leader in history since the time of the Reformation. Until the 1700s, laypeople could not serve in any type of ministry position in the church. They were exempt from teaching, visiting the sick, or holding a leadership role in the church. Clergy were the only ones who had the authority to teach or preach in the church. As a result of Wesley's decision to begin to use lay ministers in the Wesleyan revival, laypeople today have an open door in most churches to share in ministry. In this regard, Wesley was a forerunner to the modern layleader revolution in the church today.

The privilege of lay ministry is extended to both male and female. As a result of John Wesley's influence, not only can unordained men serve in the church, but women can also participate in ministry in many contemporary Christian traditions. They serve the church in many capacities: as counselors, teachers, preachers, evangelists and much more. As a result of Wesley's use of laywomen preachers, women now have the same rights and privileges as men to become ordained ministers in many denominations today. Wesley can remind us of the need for both men and women for Christian service in our churches.

Character of a Methodist

Please don't overlook this section if you are not a Methodist. I want to show that Wesley was not referring to any one particular denomination, but to all true Christians everywhere. He was much more inclusive than many people think. John Wesley wrote a tract on the *Character of a Methodist*, where he offered several marks of true Christianity that would distinguish them from the world, not from other Christians. He said, "By these marks, by these fruits of a living faith, do we labor to distinguish ourselves from the unbelieving world. But from real Christians, of whatsoever denomination they be, we earnestly desire not to be distinguished at all."[3]

These marks are not distinctively Methodist—they are the marks of genuine Christianity in all ages. Wesley's vision was not denominational; rather, it was a universal vision of what a genuine Christian should be like in every Christian denomination.

The distinguishing marks of a Methodist are not opinions of any sort. Wesley said of opinions that do not strike at the root of Christianity, we should think and let think. This refers to theological views or ideas that are not essentials of the faith. Opinions are like faces—everybody has one. But with issues such as doctrinal essentials, Wesley was unwavering. We can find a greater sense of unity and freedom with others in the body of Christ if we realize that it's OK if everybody doesn't look, think and act alike.

Wesley said, "All men will not see all things alike. It is unavoidable consequence of the present weakness and shortness of human understanding that several men will be of several minds, in religion as well as common life."[4] With essentials there should be unity, but with nonessentials, we can allow diversity. With this in mind we can say with Wesley, "Think and let think."

A Methodist is one who has "the love of God shed abroad in his heart by the Holy Ghost given unto him" (see Romans 5:5); one who "loves the Lord his God with all his heart, and with all his soul, and with all his mind, and with all his strength" (See Mark 12:30). True Christianity is marked by love toward the God of heaven and earth. It begins and ends with a loving relationship with Jesus Christ.

Anyone who claims to be a Christian yet doesn't love God is a liar. You cannot be a child of God without loving God with all of your heart, mind, soul and strength. As a result, we should be happy in God. The Westminster Confession says that we were created to glorify and enjoy God forever. True Christianity is marked by a sincere happiness and joy that God alone can give. Apart from Him, there is no happiness.

A true Methodist "prays without ceasing" (see 1 Thessalonians 5:17). They are "always to pray, and not to faint" (see Luke 18:1). One of the greatest hallmarks of the Christian faith is prayer. Wesley was a man of prayer who encouraged his followers to pray daily. He emphasized that prayer is one of the chief means of grace that God uses to draw us closer to Him. Without prayer, we cannot know God or His will for our lives. We must pray daily in order to be all that we can be for God. It has been said that to be much for God, you must be much with God. Wesley was both.

> In this he is never hindered, much less interrupted, by any person or thing. In retirement or company, in leisure, business, or conversation, his heart is ever with the Lord. Whether he lie down or rise up, God is in all his thoughts; he walks with God continually, having the loving eye of his mind still fixed upon Him, and everywhere seeing Him that is invisible.[5]

In the same way that we are to love God, we should also love our neighbor as ourselves. We should do good to all people, to neighbors and strangers, friends and enemies. Loving God is not enough. The Bible says, "Whoso hath the world's good, and seeth his

brother have need, and shutteth up his bowels of compassion from him, how dwelleth the love of God in
him?" (1 John 3:17). This means we should demon-
strate our love toward our neighbors by doing all the
good we can to all those who are in need. We should
be willing to spend and be spent for the sake of others.
It is too easy in our modern culture to simply forget
our responsibility to neighbors.

A Methodist is pure in heart. The love of God has puri-
fied his or her heart from all revengeful passions, from
envy, malice and wrath—from every unkind thought
or feeling. We are to walk before God in holiness of
heart and life. Our hearts should be pure before the
Lord, having been cleansed by the precious blood of
Jesus. We are to walk daily with God in holiness. We
should ask the Lord to forgive us from all our sins so
that we can walk before Him with a pure heart and
mind. Matthew's Gospel says, "Blessed are the pure in
heart: for they shall see God" (5:8). Purity of heart
actually draws us closer to God and prepares us for
our heavenly home. Wesley believed that every believer
could have a pure heart and pure hands.

Wesley asked the question, "Is thy heart right, as
my heart is with thine? I ask no further question. If it
be, give me thy hand. For opinions, or terms, let us
not destroy the work of God. Dost thou love and
serve God? It is enough. I give thee the right hand of
fellowship."[6]

He believed that if believers loved God with all of
their heart, mind and soul, then God would direct
them in all of their ways. Rather than giving up on others, we should allow room for God to move in people's
lives. There is too much division in the body of Christ;

Wesley can show us a model for reconciliation between Christian traditions. He was able to see what was good in other traditions and use them for his benefit. Although we don't always see alike, we can agree on the essentials of the faith and join together with common cause to fight the battles that come from outside the church.

Holiness

Lastly, Wesley can remind us that the doctrine of holiness needs to be recovered in the church today. Many churches emphasize power without purity. There can be no power where there is no purity. Many Christians today emphasize the gifts and fruit of the Spirit without taking into consideration the ethical responsibilities that come with these gifts from God. The Holy Spirit that bestows the gifts upon believers is holy and demands that we be holy (see 1 Peter 1:15, 16). The gifts of the Spirit should, in turn, make us holy. The baptism of the Holy Spirit should be seen first as empowerment to live a godly life, and secondly as empowerment for service.

Too often there is a misunderstanding of the doctrine of holiness, and no one has misunderstood it more than the church. It has been the cause of countless splits within Christianity. The sad fact is that many Christians are either legalistic or libertarian. True holiness is neither. God calls His children to be different in a way that reaches out to the world in a relevant way without compromising the Christian faith. People should be able to see that there is something different about our lives. This, of course, does not mean the way we dress or the length of our hair; rather, holiness is a way of life that is different from the way of the world.

The people of God must be a "contrast-society," who by their life should always hold in tension separation from the culture and loving the culture.[7] This is an area where the church often misunderstands her role and calling to be salt and light (Matthew 5:13, 14). There is a need to explore what it means to have holiness in the marketplace. It is important for the church to rethink its interpretation of holiness as a dialogue between church and culture in order to remain relevant in a postmodern world. True holiness must always be a response to the culture—both in love and separation, resulting in individual and social holiness.

Lessons for Today

These are but a few ways the church can learn from the life, ministry and message of John Wesley. In no way is this an exhaustive list; rather, these are some small suggestions toward a rediscovery of Wesley. There are many contributions he can make to the church in areas of human rights, which include issues of racial equality, caring for the poor and equal rights for women.

He can also contribute toward the ecumenical movement by pleading for unity of all believers in issues of essentials, not opinions. He offers the church a model for personal, local and global evangelism. He challenges the church in the area of stewardship. Many Christians in debt desperately need to have a balanced view of Christian finances. Finally, he offers a balanced perspective of Christian holiness.

REFLECTION QUESTIONS

1. What do you think is the single most important contribution of John Wesley today?

2. Which one do you think the church needs to rediscover most? Explain why.

3. What do you think is the most important thing about Christian stewardship?

4. Have you ever thought that Christians should handle their money differently than non-Christians?

5. In what ways do you think Wesley contributed most toward empowerment of lay members?

6. Do you think your church needs to rethink its stance on helping the poor?

Endnotes

[1] "Use of Money" *Works*, 6:133.

[2] Robert Coleman, *Nothing to Do but to Save Souls: John Wesley's Charge to His Preachers* (Grand Rapids: Francis Asbury, 1990).

[3] *Works*, 8:346.

[4] *Works*, 5:494.

[5] *Works*, 8:343.

[6] Gerhard Lohfink says the church's role in contemporary society is to serve as a "contrast-society." "This model has tremendous missional promise: it reminds the church that its witness to the world is not something separate from its own embodied existence in the midst of the world. The church must attend to the character of its embodied life because that embodied life is its witness to the world." Phillip D. Kenneson, *Beyond Sectarianism: Re-Imaging Church and World* (Harrisburg, PA: Trinity, 1989) 2.

[7] *Works*, 8:347.

Conclusion

In conclusion, I would like to summarize the contents and emphasize the importance of this book. John Wesley has been known as the theological ancestor of many movements, but many who are within these traditions are unaware of unique contributions that he can continue to offer. Wesley's life was an amazing example of what God can do through a willing vessel. He offered his life freely to people he served. He was a great preacher, religious leader, theologian, and friend to many. We can continue to learn from this giant of a man who stood only about five feet tall.

Wesley's theology was both relevant and practical. He desired to teach and preach in such a way that the people could understand and respond to the grace of God. Wesley's theological method offers us insight into his practical theology. Perhaps the most important and seemingly overlooked of all is the role of the Holy Spirit in each of the four areas of religious authority. The Spirit of God is both the Agent and the Divine Interpreter of the religious sources. For Wesley, Scripture, reason, tradition, and experience are only affective through the accompanied presence and activity of the Holy Spirit. The Spirit serves as the guide through these four areas. The Wesleyan Quadrilateral offers us an approach to theology in which we can encounter the living God.

Wesley also offers us various ways and approaches to ministry in every day life. He was on the cutting edge of his day and was willing to use whatever means necessary to save souls and keep them on the way to perfection. His evangelistic efforts were daring and most effective. Perhaps even more importantly was his ability and insight to place people into covenant groups that would help new and old believers continue to keep pressing on in the Christian faith. Small groups are probably the single most important ministry praxis that he gave the church. Along with these was his concern for social and benevolence ministries. He cared for the poor and disenfranchised of society. He can challenge us to take the gospel to the world by whatever means necessary.

Another important aspect of Wesley's life and theology is the call for holiness. The Christian faith is based on loving God and neighbor. In loving God, the Christian is set apart from the world and sin. In loving our neighbor, we are sent back into the world as sanctified persons with a missionary love for the lost. Love creates a missionary zeal for God and the world. True holiness must always be a paradox of love and separation. Because we love, we live our lives dedicated to the beauty of holiness unto our God. This love allows us to be missionaries to the world around us because we have been sanctified, set apart, and made holy as God is holy. In the end we can learn a lot from John Wesley as we look toward the future of Christianity.

Finally, we can see the lasting influence of Wesley's legacy in the various Wesleyan Christian traditions, many of which do not know much about their ancestor. A close look at the statistical growth of these movements after Wesley's death testifies to his amazing leadership. He sought to reform Anglicanism, but ended up directly influencing most of modern Christianity, both Catholic and Protestant. One of his most significant contributions is also one of the most forgotten: Pentecostalism. His emphasis on the role of the Holy Spirit in Christian experience and sanctification helped create a major paradigm shift in North American Christianity that resulted in the formation of Pentecostalism. His ministry and message can provide a helpful model to address some of the universal issues that are still facing the church today.

The marks of a Methodist are universal principles that should be demonstrated in the lives of all believers throughout all ages, no matter what the church background; whether Wesleyan, Baptist, Pentecostal, or non-denominational.

part four

Appendixes and Study Aids

* * * * * * *

Glossary

Antinomian—Literally means "against the law." It is a teaching that maintains Christians are free from the law of God by the grace of God.

Assurance—The confidence that we are children of God through the inner witness of the Holy Spirit.

Class Meeting—Small group of Methodists who gathered weekly for fellowship, prayer and Bible study.

Justification—An unmerited act of God where a sinful person is declared "just" on the merits of Jesus Christ.

Means of Grace—Means of conveying the grace of God. "Outward sign, words, or actions, ordained of God, and appointed for this end, to be the ordinary channels whereby he might convey to men, preventing, justifying, or sanctifying grace" (Wesley).

Ordo Salutis—The order of the process of salvation (justification, regeneration, sanctification).

Prevenient Grace—Literally means the grace of God that operates before conversion. It is the Holy Spirit who works in the hearts of men and women to make it possible to accept God's free gift of salvation.

Regeneration—The act of the Holy Spirit transforming the lives of those who have become Christians through faith in Jesus Christ. It is also called "salvation" and "new birth."

Repentance—Refers to the conviction of sin that produces a real change of mind and life in persons toward God.

Sacraments—Outward signs given by God to convey an inward work of grace.

Sanctification—The process of God's work in a believer that begins at the new birth, in which Christians are saved from the power and root of sin, and restored to the image of God.

Wesleyan Quadrilateral—Literally, a four-sided figure. Refers to sources that John Wesley used to come to doctrinal truth. The four areas of the Wesleyan Quadrilateral: Scripture, tradition, reason, and experience, while Scripture is considered primary.

Time Line of Wesley's Life

June 17, 1703	Wesley's birth
February 9, 1709	Parsonage at Epworth burned
January 28, 1714	Entered Charterhouse School
June 24, 1720	Entered Christ College of Oxford University
September 19, 1725	Ordained deacon, Anglican Church
March 17, 1726	Elected fellowship at Lincoln College
February 14, 1727	Received M.A. at Oxford
November 22, 1729	Joined the Holy Club
October 14, 1735	Sailed for Georgia
December 22, 1737	Returned to England
May 24, 1738	Aldersgate experience
April 1, 1739	Began field preaching, Bristol

December 1739	Methodist Society at the Foundry
February 18 or 19, 1751	Married widow Mary Vazeille
October 8, 1781	Death of his wife, Mary
March 29, 1788	Death of Charles Wesley
March 2, 1791	John Wesley dies. His last words: "Best of all, God is with us."

Important People and Places in Wesley's Life

People

Francis Asbury—American Methodist bishop sent by Wesley

Peter Bohler—Moravian leader and acquaintance

Sophey Hopkey—a former love interest in Georgia who married another man

Robert Strawbridge—first Methodist preacher in America

Mary Vazeille—widow who married John

Charles Wesley—younger brother of John; close friend and ministry associate

Samuel Wesley—father of the Wesleys

Susanna Wesley—mother of John and Charles

George Whitefield—close friend and associate of John Wesley; introduced John to field preaching

Count Zinzendorf—leader of the Moravians

Places

Aldersgate Street, London—place where John had his heart-warming experience

Charterhouse—London school that John attended for six years

City Road Chapel, London—John Wesley's burial place

Epworth—place where John Wesley was born

Foundry—early meetinghouse for Wesley and Moravian societies

Lincoln College—college where John had a fellowship

New Room, Bristol—first chapel of Wesley's societies

Savannah, GA—place where John served as a missionary

Wesley Quotes

"I desire plain truth for plain people."

"It matters not how long we live, but how well."

"But as to all opinions which do not strike at the root of Christianity, we think and let think."

"I am not afraid that the people called Methodists should ever cease to exist either in Europe or America. But I am afraid, lest they should only exist as a dead sect, having the form of religion without the power."

"I look upon all the world as my parish."

"Is thy heart right, as my heart is with thine? I ask no farther question. If it be, give me thy hand. For opinions, or terms, let us not destroy the work of God. Dost thou love and serve God? It is enough. I give thee the right hand of fellowship."

"The soul and the body make the man; and the spirit and discipline make a Christian."

"The gospel of Christ knows no religion but social, no holiness but social holiness."

"Gain all you can, save all you can, so you can give all you can."

"Do all the good you can;
By all the means you can;
In all the places you can;
At all the times you can;
To all the people you can;
As long as you ever can."

"Best of all, God is with us."

Articles of Religion

The following Articles of Religion were a set of doctrinal statements that John Wesley sent to America with his *Sunday Service* in 1784. They are a revision of the Anglican 39 Articles of Religion. He revised them to 24 and sent them to American Methodists as doctrinal standard for them to follow. The American Methodist Church added an additional one recognizing America as a free and sovereign country, making it 25.

Article I—Of Faith in the Holy Trinity

There is but one living and true God, everlasting, without body or parts, of infinite power, wisdom, and goodness; the maker and preserver of all things, both visible and invisible. And in unity of this Godhead there are three persons, of one substance, power, and eternity—the Father, the Son, and the Holy Ghost.

Article II—Of the Word, or Son of God, Who Was Made Very Man

The Son, who is the Word of the Father, the very and eternal God, of one substance with the Father, took man's nature in the womb of the blessed Virgin; so that two whole and perfect natures, that is to say, the Godhead and Manhood, were joined together in one person, never to be divided; whereof is one Christ, very God and very Man, who truly suffered, was crucified, dead, and buried, to reconcile his Father to us, and to be a sacrifice, not only for original guilt, but also for actual sins of men.

Article III—Of the Resurrection of Christ

Christ did truly rise again from the dead, and took again his body, with all things appertaining to the perfection of man's nature, wherewith he ascended into heaven, and there sitteth until he return to judge all men at the last day.

Article IV—Of the Holy Ghost

The Holy Ghost, proceeding from the Father and the Son, is of one substance, majesty, and glory with the Father and the Son, very and eternal God.

Article V—Of the Sufficiency of the Holy Scriptures for Salvation

The Holy Scripture containeth all things necessary to salvation; so that whatsoever is not read therein, nor may be proved thereby, is not to be required of any man that it should be believed as an article of faith, or be thought requisite or necessary to salvation. In the name of the Holy Scripture we do understand those canonical books of the Old and New Testament of whose authority was never any doubt in the church. The names of the canonical books are:

> Genesis, Exodus, Leviticus, Numbers, Deuteronomy, Joshua, Judges, Ruth, The First Book of Samuel, The Second Book of Samuel, The First Book of Kings, The Second Book of Kings, The First Book of Chronicles, The Second Book of Chronicles, The Book of Ezra, The Book of Nehemiah, The Book of Esther, The Book of Job, The Psalms, The Proverbs, Ecclesiastes or the Preacher, Cantica or Songs of Solomon, Four Prophets the Greater, Twelve Prophets the Less.

All the books of the New Testament, as they are commonly received, we do receive and account canonical.

Article VI—Of the Old Testament

The Old Testament is not contrary to the New; for both in the Old and New Testament everlasting life is offered to mankind by Christ, who is the only Mediator between God and man, being both God and Man. Wherefore they are not to be heard who feign that the old fathers did look only for transitory promises. Although the law given from God by Moses as touching ceremonies and rites doth not bind Christians, nor ought the civil precepts thereof of necessity be received in any commonwealth; yet notwithstanding, no Christian whatsoever is free from the obedience of the commandments which are called moral.

Article VII—Of Original or Birth Sin

Original sin standeth not in the following of Adam (as the Pelagians do vainly talk), but it is the corruption of the nature of every man, that naturally is engendered of the offspring of Adam, whereby man is very far gone from original righteousness, and of his own nature inclined to evil, and that continually.

Article VIII—Of Free Will

The condition of man after the fall of Adam is such that he cannot turn and prepare himself, by his own natural strength and works, to faith, and calling upon God; wherefore we have no power to do good works, pleasant and acceptable to God, without the grace of God by Christ preventing us, that we may have a good will, and working with us, when we have that good will.

Article IX—Of the Justification of Man

We are accounted righteous before God only for the

merit of our Lord and Saviour Jesus Christ, by faith, and not for our own works or deservings. Wherefore, that we are justified by faith, only, is a most wholesome doctrine, and very full of comfort.

Article X—Of Good Works

Although good works, which are the fruits of faith, and follow after justification, cannot put away our sins, and endure the severity of God's judgment; yet are they pleasing and acceptable to God in Christ, and spring out of a true and lively faith, insomuch that by them a lively faith may be as evidently known as a tree is discerned by its fruit.

Article XI—Of Works of Supererogation

Voluntary works—besides, over and above God's commandments—which they call works of supererogation, cannot be taught without arrogancy and impiety. For by them men do declare that they do not only render unto God as much as they are bound to do, but that they do more for his sake than of bounden duty is required; whereas Christ saith plainly: "When you have done all that is commanded you, say, We are unprofitable servants."

Article XII—Of Sin After Justification

Not every sin willingly committed after justification is the sin against the Holy Ghost, and unpardonable. Wherefore, the grant of repentance is not to be denied to such as fall into sin after justification. After we have received the Holy Ghost, we may depart from grace given, and fall into sin, and, by the grace of God, rise again and amend our lives. And therefore they are to be condemned who say they can no more sin as long as they live here; or deny the place of forgiveness to such as truly repent.

Article XIII—Of the Church

The visible church of Christ is a congregation of faithful men in which the pure Word of God is preached, and the Sacraments duly administered according to Christ's ordinance, in all those things that of necessity are requisite to the same.

Article XIV—Of Purgatory

The Romish doctrine concerning purgatory, pardon, worshiping, and adoration, as well of images as of relics, and also invocation of saints, is a fond thing, vainly invented, and grounded upon no warrant of Scripture, but repugnant to the Word of God.

Article XV—Of Speaking in the Congregation in Such a Tongue as the People Understand

It is a thing plainly repugnant to the Word of God, and the custom of the primitive church, to have public prayer in the church, or to minister the Sacraments, in a tongue not understood by the people.

Article XVI—Of the Sacraments

Sacraments ordained of Christ are not only badges or tokens of Christian men's profession, but rather they are certain signs of grace, and God's good will toward us, by which he doth work invisibly in us, and doth not only quicken, but also strengthen and confirm, our faith in him.

There are two Sacraments ordained of Christ our Lord in the Gospel; that is to say, Baptism and the Supper of the Lord.

Those five commonly called sacraments, that is to say, confirmation, penance, orders, matrimony, and extreme unction, are not to be counted for Sacraments of the Gospel; being such as have partly grown out of the corrupt following of the apostles, and partly are states of life allowed in the Scriptures, but yet have not the like nature of Baptism and the Lord's Supper, because they have not any visible sign or ceremony ordained of God.

The Sacraments were not ordained of Christ to be gazed upon, or to be carried about; but that we should duly use them. And in such only as worthily receive the same, they have a wholesome effect or operation; but they that receive them unworthily, purchase to themselves condemnation, as St. Paul saith.

Article XVII—Of Baptism

Baptism is not only a sign of profession and mark of difference whereby Christians are distinguished from others that are not baptized; but it is also a sign of regeneration or the new birth. The Baptism of young children is to be retained in the Church.

Article XVIII—Of the Lord's Supper

The Supper of the Lord is not only a sign of the love that Christians ought to have among themselves one to another, but rather is a sacrament of our redemption by Christ's death; insomuch that, to such as rightly, worthily, and with faith receive the same, the bread which we break is a partaking of the body of Christ; and likewise the cup of blessing is a partaking of the blood of Christ.

Transubstantiation, or the change of the substance of bread and wine in the Supper of our Lord, cannot be proved by Holy Writ, but is repugnant to the plain words of Scripture, overthroweth the nature of a sacrament, and hath given occasion to many superstitions.

The body of Christ is given, taken, and eaten in the Supper, only after a heavenly and spiritual manner. And the means whereby the body of Christ is received and eaten in the Supper is faith.

The Sacrament of the Lord's Supper was not by Christ's ordinance reserved, carried about, lifted up, or worshiped.

Article XIX—Of Both Kinds

The cup of the Lord is not to be denied to the lay people; for both the parts of the Lord's Supper, by Christ's ordinance and commandment, ought to be administered to all Christians alike.

Article XX—Of the One Oblation of Christ, Finished Upon the Cross

The offering of Christ, once made, is that perfect redemption, propitiation, and satisfaction for all the sins of the whole world, both original and actual; and there is none other satisfaction for sin but that alone. Wherefore the sacrifice of masses, in the which it is commonly said that the priest doth offer Christ for the quick and the dead, to have remission of pain or guilt, is a blasphemous fable and dangerous deceit.

Article XXI—Of the Marriage of Ministers

The ministers of Christ are not commanded by God's law either to vow the estate of single life, or to abstain from marriage; therefore it is lawful for them, as for all other Christians, to marry at their own discretion, as they shall judge the same to serve best to godliness.

Article XXII—Of the Rites and Ceremonies of Churches

It is not necessary that rites and ceremonies should in all places be the same, or exactly alike; for they have been always different, and may be changed according to the diversity of countries, times, and men's manners, so that nothing be ordained against God's Word. Whosoever, through his private judgment, willingly and purposely doth openly break the rites and ceremonies of the church to which he belongs, which are not repugnant to the Word of God, and are ordained and approved by common authority, ought to be rebuked openly, that others may fear to do the like, as one that offendeth against the common order of the church, and woundeth the consciences of weak brethren.

Every particular church may ordain, change, or abolish rites and ceremonies, so that all things may be done to edification.

Article XXIII—Of the Rulers of the United States of America

The President, the Congress, the general assemblies, the governors, and the councils of state, as the delegates of the people, are the rulers of the United States of America, according to the division of power made to them by the Constitution of the United States and by the constitutions of their respective states. And the said states are a sovereign and independent nation, and ought not to be subject to any foreign jurisdiction.

Article XXIV—Of Christian Men's Goods

The riches and goods of Christians are not common as touching the right, title, and possession of the same, as some do falsely boast. Notwithstanding, every man ought, of such things as he possesseth, liberally to give alms to the poor, according to his ability.

Article XXV—Of a Christian Man's Oath

As we confess that vain and rash swearing is forbidden Christian men by our Lord Jesus Christ and James his apostle, so we judge that the Christian religion doth not prohibit, but that a man may swear when the magistrate requireth, in a cause of faith and charity, so it be done according to the prophet's teaching, in justice, judgment, and truth.

Wesleyan Bibliography

Primary Sources

Baker, Frank, ed. *The Works of John Wesley.* Bicentennial ed. 34 vols. Nashville: Abingdon, 1976.

Curnock, Nehemiah, ed. *The Journal of Rev. John Wesley.* 8 vols. London: Epworth, 1909-1916.

Jackson, Thomas, ed. *The Works of Rev. John Wesley.* 14 vols. London: Wesleyan Methodist Book Room, 1829-1831. Reprinted, Grand Rapids: Baker, 1978.

————, ed. *The Journals of Rev. Charles Wesley.* 2 vols. London: John Mason, 1949. Reprinted, Grand Rapids: Baker, 1980.

Kimbrough, S.T. Jr., and Oliver A. Beckerlegge, eds. *The Unpublished Poetry of Charles Wesley.* Nashville: Abingdon, 1993.

————. *The Unpublished Poetical Writings of Charles Wesley.* 3 vols. Nashville: Kingswood, 1988-1992.

Outler, Albert C., ed. *John Wesley.* New York: Oxford UP, 1964.

———, ed. *The Works of John Wesley*. Bicentennial ed. Vols. 1-4: Sermons. Nashville: Abingdon, 1984-1987.

Outler, Albert C., and Richard P. Heitzenrater, eds. *John Wesley's Sermons: An Anthology*. Nashville: Abingdon, 1991.

Parker, Percy L., ed. *The Journal of John Wesley*. Chicago: Moody, 1974.

Sugden, Edward H., ed. *Wesley's Standard Sermons*. London: Epworth, 1951.

Telford, John, ed. *The Letters of the Rev. John Wesley*. 8 vols. London: Epworth, 1931.

———, ed. *Sayings and Portraits of John Wesley*. Salem, OH: Schmul, 1995.

Wainwright, Geoffrey, ed. *Hymns on the Lord's Supper*. Madison, NJ: Charles Wesley Society, 1995.

Wesley, Charles. *The Journal of the Rev. Charles Wesley*. 2 vols. Ed. Thomas Jackson. London: John Mason, 1849. Reprint, Kansas City, MO: Beacon Hill, 1980.

Wesley, John. *Explanatory Notes Upon the New Testament*. London: William Bowyer, 1755. Most recent reprint, Grand Rapids: Baker, 1987.

———. *Explanatory Notes Upon the Old Testament*. 3 vols. Bristol: William Pine, 1765. Facsimile reprint, Salem, OH: Schmul, 1975.

White, James F., ed. *John Wesley's Prayer Book: The Sunday Service of the Methodists in North America*. Cleveland, OH: OSL Publications, 1991.

Secondary Sources

Ayling, Stanley. *John Wesley.* Nashville: Abingdon, 1979.

Campbell, Ted A. John Wesley and Christian Antiquity: Religious Vision and Cultural Change. Nashville: Kingswood, 1991.

Cannon, William R. *The Theology of John Wesley.* Nashville: Abingdon, 1946.

Coleman, Robert E. "Nothing to Do but to Save Souls." *John Wesley's Charge to His Preachers.* Grand Rapids: Francis Asbury, 1990.

Collins, Kenneth J. *A Real Christian: The Life of John Wesley.* Nashville: Abingdon, 1999.

————. *The Scripture Way of Salvation: The Heart of John Wesley's Theology.* Nashville: Abingdon, 1997.

————. "John Wesley's Critical Appropriation of Tradition in His Practical Theology." *Wesleyan Theological Journal* 35:2 (2000).

Davies, Rupert, A. Raymond George, and Gordon Rupp, eds. A History of the Methodist Church in Great Britain. Vol. 4. London: Epworth, 1998.

Greathouse, William M. *From the Apostles to Wesley: Christian Perfection in Historical Perspective.* Kansas City, MO: Beacon Hill, 1979.

Green, V.H.H. *The Young Mr. Wesley.* London: Edward Arnold, 1961.

Heitzenrater, Richard P. *The Elusive Mr. Wesley.* 2 vols. Nashville: Abingdon, 1984.

————. *Wesley and the People Called Methodists.* Nashville: Abingdon, 1995.

Henderson, D. Michael. *John Wesley's Class Meeting: A Model for Making Disciples.* Nappanee, IN: Evangel, 1997.

Jackson, Thomas, ed. *Works of John Wesley.* Grand Rapids: Baker, 1979.

Langford, Thomas A. *Practical Divinity: Theology in the Wesleyan Tradition.* Nashville: Abingdon, 1983.

Maddox, Randy L. *Responsible Grace: John Wesley's Practical Theology.* Nashville: Kingwood, 1994.

Oden, Thomas C. *John Wesley's Scriptural Christianity: A Plain Exposition of His Teaching on Christian Doctrine.* Grand Rapids: Zondervan, 1994.

Outler, Albert C. "A Focus on the Holy Spirit: Spirit and Spirituality in John Wesley." *Quarterly Review* (1988).

————. *John Wesley.* New York: Oxford UP, 1964.

————. "The Wesleyan Quadrilateral in John Wesley." *Wesleyan Theological Journal* 20:1 (Spring, 1985).

————. *Theology in the Wesleyan Spirit.* Nashville: Discipleship Resources, 1975.

Schmidt, Martin. *John Wesley: A Theological Biography.* 3 vols. Nashville: Abingdon, 1960.

Snyder, Howard A. *The Radical Wesley: Pattern for Church Renewal*. Grand Rapids: Zondervan, 1987.

Telford, John. *The Life of John Wesley*. London: Wesleyan Methodist Book Room, 1899.

Thorsen, Donald A.D. *The Wesleyan Quadrilateral: Scripture, Tradition, Reason, and Experience as a Model of Evangelical Theology*. Grand Rapids: Zondervan, 1990.

Tuttle, Robert G. *John Wesley: His Life and Theology*. Grand Rapids: Zondervan, 1982.

Williams, Colin W. *John Wesley's Theology Today*. Nashville: Abingdon, 1960.

Wood, Lawrence W. "Pentecostal Sanctification in John Wesley and Early Methodism." *Wesleyan Theological Journal* 34:1 (1999).

———. The Meaning of Pentecost in Early Methodism: Rediscovering John Fletcher as Wesley's Vindicator and Designated Successor. Lanham, MD: Scarecrow, 2003.

Wood, Skevington. *The Burning Heart: John Wesley, Evangelist*. Minneapolis: Bethany, 1978.

Wynkoop, Mildred Bangs. *A Theology of Love: The Dynamic of Wesleyanism*. Kansas City, MO: Beacon Hill, 1972.